D1095021

MEAD AND WINE

JEAN ZAFIROPULO

MEAD AND WINE

A HISTORY OF THE BRONZE AGE IN GREECE

Translated from the French by

PETER GREEN

SIDGWICK AND JACKSON
LONDON
1966

First published in this translation by Sidgwick & Jackson Ltd. in 1966

Printed in Great Britain by Billing & Sons Ltd., Guildford and London

Contents

Acknowledgments

The various plates illustrating this book have been reproduced by the kind permission of:

The American School of Classical Studies in Athens

The American School of Classical Studies in Corinth

Editions du Griffon, La Neuveville, Switzerland (*Dialectica*)

Doctor N. Platon

Doctor N. M. Verdelis

The German Archaeological Institute of Athens

The Greek Archaeological Society

The Hirmer Verlag

Professor R. Blegen

Professor V. R. d'A. Desborough

List of Sketches and Tables

List of Plates

Prefatory Note

It was Paul Tannery who led me to investigate the Pre-Socratics, and the German Occupation that gave me the time to begin writing. My research on Zeno and Parmenides brought me up against a problem which the Greeks were unable to solve: must the language used to describe the world be one presupposing continuity or discontinuity?

This problem soon becomes mathematical, and, indeed, embodies the whole problem of epistemological knowledge. Today, despite appearances, our theories remain axiomatic, and thus *a priori*. We construct them first and try to verify them afterwards. Thus the language we choose to employ, whether continuous or discontinuous, can be varied according to our whim, and truth becomes a definition, modified by the passage of time and the axioms admitted in any given period.

I wrote the history of these various modifications in a book called *Vox Zenonis*, beginning with Pythagoras and proceeding, by way of Aristotle, Newton, Einstein, and De Broglie, to Kurt Goedel's demonstration that there can be no axiomatic theory which does not contain at least one contradiction, and therefore that no theory can ever hope to be definitive.

Afterwards I came to realise that each natural philosophy, each physical world one constructed in this way, could have one corresponding metaphysical firmament above it, and one only: in other words, that all formal symbols which we adopt in the sphere of reason are equally binding in the sphere of irrational generalisation—that generalisation which sets man and his destiny within the framework of an ineluctable aesthetic pattern. All this, though not evident, is nevertheless inevitable.

Meanwhile I had made the acquaintance of Jean Charon, whose ideas on continuity and discontinuity opened up fresh horizons for me. I therefore rewrote my book *Vox Zenonis*, extending every physical concept to include its metaphysical counterpart, and embodying

Charon's latest theories in the text. I called this new essay *Apollo and Dionysus*, to symbolise the necessary union, at every step we take, of the rational (our modern mathematics) and the irrational, of the lawgiver and the bringer of ecstasy.

Quite arbitrarily, I took the Delphic solution of the problem of knowlege as my departure-point, both because my previous researches on the Pre-Socratics had familiarised me with it, and because I was thus enabled to begin with Pythagoras, who is, by and large, the father of modern epistemological method.

But this departure-point remained arbitrary nevertheless, and logically speaking it was essential to push it back as far into the past as possible, right back to the earliest mythical solutions of the problem which have been preserved to the present day. Then Ventris deciphered the Mycenean script known as Linear B, which dates from the Greek Bronze Age. With this new line of approach now available, was it possible to thrust back the frontiers of our knowledge yet further, to build on foundations a thousand years older than those of Delphi? A deep and detailed examination of the question convinced me that it *was* possible. Both Apollo and Dionysus had a long history behind them when they first appeared at Delphi.

This book is an attempt to reconstruct that history, from their humble beginnings to their final ascendancy. Now, I feel, the chain of development is complete. From the first Achaean shepherds to Jean Charon the history of cognition develops in an unbroken sequence. I would like this book to be read as an introduction to the more complex problems of *Apollo and Dionysus*; it forms, as it were, their prolegomena.

CHAPTER I

Problems of Chronology: Dating the Greek Bronze Age Dynasties

OUR evidence for the Bronze Age in Greece and Crete derives from several sources.[1] We have, first, the contemporary sources—the results, that is, of our interpretation of archaeological digs, and also of the Linear B tablets: reading them has enabled us to catch a living glimpse of certain aspects of Greek and Cretan civilisation at the end of the Bronze Age. Next, we have the Homeric poems, which in the eighth century B.C. crystallised a mass of ancient traditional folklore, handed down orally from the Mycenean period:[2] this was the tradition upon which Schliemann relied to show the world that—despite the Dark Ages—the legends men had preserved, though often somewhat fantastic, nevertheless contained, in the last resort, a good deal more historical truth than anyone was then disposed to admit.[3] We also possess various non-Greek chronological records, in particular those Egyptian and Hittite ones which refer to contact with the Cretan and Achaean peoples,[4] together with various passages from the Hebrew scriptures. Finally we have the myths, in particular the most ancient versions of them as preserved in Homer,[5] Hesiod, and various poets—Pindar, for instance, and the tragedians. All the evidence suggests that this source should be utilised with great circumspection; yet it too would appear to contain a core of historical truth which is not beyond being worked into an approximate date-scheme. Nor must we neglect the testimony of ancient historians, in particular Thucydides and Herodotus, who have preserved what was still remembered in their day, and Pausanias, who not only set down accurate descriptions of the monuments surviving during his lifetime, but also recorded the legends associated with them. I shall, as the occasion arises, utilise these and other sources which can cast some light on the subject under discussion.

Hesiod in particular, I feel, has often been unjustly neglected by historians. He must have been a near-contemporary of Homer, and the very complexity of the myths and genealogies which he determined seems sure proof that he did not make them up himself. Besides, had he done so he could never have persuaded anyone of their authenticity: they must, in fact, have been based on an extremely ancient folk-tradition. It is more than likely that this congeries, like the Homeric tradition, contains many details dating back to the period with which we are here concerned. Here, for instance, is what Hesiod has to tell us about the Greeks of the Bronze Age: they had bronze weapons, their houses were of bronze, they tilled the earth with bronze ploughshares, they did not eat bread, they died by their own hand, and went to dwell in the dank realm of Hades, leaving no name behind them.[6] As we shall see, the tradition which Hesiod here records is correct in every detail. The house of bronze is the third temple at Delphi, built by Cadmus and covered with bronze plates, which still survived in Pausanias's day. Bread was, in fact, unknown at this period; and the Achaeans did perish at each others' hands, in a terrible religious war, without any external intervention worthy of note—neither Homer nor Hesiod appears to be acquainted with the Dorians.[7] Finally, the very fact that these Bronze Age men had existed at all was forgotten—until the day when, before the astonished eyes of the world, Schliemann and Evans disinterred their remains.

Our knowledge in all these fields of evidence has recently taken great strides forward. The most spectacular achievement, of course, has been Ventris's decipherment of the Linear B tablets.[8] 'The history of Greece and of Greek culture', Wace wrote,[9] 'will have to be rewritten from the outlook of our present knowledge, and as more pre-Classical texts are found and deciphered, so our knowledge will grow. . . . A fresh examination of the legends of early Greece must also be undertaken to estimate their archaeological and historical value.' This book attempts such an evaluation of the historical credibility of myths from the period known as Late Helladic III—that is, myths roughly datable between 1400 and 1100 B.C., a time-span which also coincides with the Late Minoan III period in Crete.

In this complex undertaking my task has, as we shall see, been greatly facilitated by the fact that the myths associated with the dynasties of Thebes, Crete, and Mycenae cover historical events which were, for the most part, both contemporary and directly interrelated. The appearance of Heracles, no less than that of the Heraclidae at Thebes, has to find some natural explanation in the general historical pattern one deduces from the facts. In particular, the double 'descent of the Heraclidae', crowned with success only at the second attempt, must be explained both historically *and* chronologically. We will also have to bear in mind the fact that the ancient world knew nothing of the famous 'Dorian invasion'; all they remembered was the 'return of the Heraclidae'.

Before embarking on a detailed discussion of how my chronological tables were constructed, I would like to make one general observation. In the Bronze Age agriculture was still relatively unimportant, and man's major source of livelihood continued to be cattle-breeding. This meant that large population movements were, practically speaking, impossible, except in the shape of tribal migrations, with the clans marching behind their cattle. Otherwise an invading population would have very soon starved to death. Thucydides's highly pertinent remarks about the deplorable commissariat of the Achaean army before Troy[10] are reflected in Sophocles' *Ajax*, where the immensity of the hero's crime derives from the fact that, in his madness, he mistook the ration-animals for the enemy, and slaughtered them.[11]

As we shall see, Achaean society, like that described by Homer, possessed very few slaves—a fact which may be explained by the shortage of food, acute enough to necessitate severe rationing. Ethnic movements in Bronze Age Greece consisted of small group migrations, and these did not so much invade new territory as infiltrate it. Furthermore, during the period with which we are here concerned, the country was very strongly defended, and governed with remarkable efficiency. Any other technique than infiltration was doomed to certain failure, and the idea of a horde of barbarous Dorians swarming over those Cyclopean walls, carrying all before them, is a myth which the ancient world never knew. The historical truth could not but be different. At the very height of their power the Greeks took ten years to reduce Troy alone; and we know that the Heraclidae never succeeded in storming the fortified Acropolis of Athens. Gla, Mycenae and Tiryns were no less powerful: why then could they not hold out likewise? We shall attempt to find an answer to all these questions; but first we must establish, as accurately as the evidence will permit, a chronological sequence for the dynasties that reigned during the Late Helladic III period.

As far as the dating of Late Minoan III is concerned, I accept the hypothesis advanced by Prof. L. R. Palmer,[12] which seems to me absolutely convincing.[13] I shall, therefore, assume with him that the Palace of Cnossos was burnt twice: once about 1405[14] by the Achaeans, who rebuilt it for their own use,[15] and a second time about 1100 by the supposed 'Dorians', who left it in ruins. For reasons which I will elaborate at length in due course, I do not believe that the appearance at Cnossos of the so-called 'Palace Style' between 1450 and 1405 corresponded to the rule of an early Greek dynasty that was then overthrown by the invasion in 1400. Theseus only slew the Minotaur once, and that was towards the close of the fifteenth century before our era. I shall return to this crucial point later, and discuss it in detail. There was no Cretan revolution about the year 1400.

For the chronology of Mycenae I base my researches on Mylonas,[16] but only in respect of the period up to *circa* 1300. Despite the arguments published by Blegen,[17] Mylonas maintains that Troy fell at the traditional date of 1183.[18] Blegen's examination of Troy VIIa[19] seems irrefutable in its conclusions, and I propose to follow it, placing the fall of Troy at 1240, which thus gives 1250 for the preparations prior to the launching of this famous campaign. Consequently the latter part of Mylonas's chronology must be back-dated by about half a century.[20]

We have now to reckon with the fact that the same leaders who fought in the campaign of the Epigoni, which brought about the fall of Thebes, also sailed on the expedition against Troy. We must, therefore, date the fall of Thebes immediately before the initial preparations for the grand expedition into Asia Minor—that is, *circa* 1250. This would mean placing the unsuccessful expedition of the Seven against Thebes half a generation earlier, since we know that the Epigoni, or Successors, were still quite young when the famous Seven were killed.[21] The expedition of the Seven against Thebes must therefore have taken place in about 1265 B.C.

The Greeks knew Perseus as the builder of Mycenae,[22] which means that we must associate him with the first ring-wall of the fortress. This first ring-wall can be dated to 1350 or thereabouts[23] which means that Perseus must have taken possession of the citadel some years previously—say between 1360 and 1355. He was beyond doubt a remarkable character: as late as the time of Herodotus cult-honours were still paid to him in Egypt.[24] Even the Persians claimed descent from him, and tried to use this supposed consanguinity as an argument to get Argive support during the second Persian War.[25]

Herodotus asserts that Perseus is the first historical individual to appear in Greek prehistory,[26] and we have no reason to cast doubt on his supposition. One point that will assume great importance later in this essay is the fact that Herodotus also tells us—during the same discussion—how Perseus was the son of Danaë,[27] and how Danaë's father

TABLE OF COMPARATIVE CHRONOLOGIES

	CRETE		GREECE		TROY	EGYPT	
2200		Early Minoan		Early Helladic			2200
2100							2100
	I				Troy V		
2000						XIIth & XIIIth dynasties	2000
1900	II						1900
	III			Middle Helladic	Troy VI		
1800	I	Middle Minoan					1800
1700	II					Hyksos	1700
1600	III						1600
			I	Late Helladic			
1500	I	Late Minoan	II			XVIIIth dynasty	1500
	II Cnossos						
1400							1400
1300							1300
	III		III		Troy VIIa	XIXth dynasty	
1200					Troy VIIb		1200
						XXth dynasty	
1100							1100

Acrisius had a great-grandfather, Danaus, who, according to tradition, was an immigrant from Egypt.[28]

There is nothing surprising about this, since Danaus's appearance in Greece would have to be placed some five generations before Perseus—that is, about the middle of the sixteenth century, which was the period when the Pharaoh Amosis, known as the Liberator, and the founder of the Eighteenth Dynasty, drove the Hyksos out of Egypt.[29] The Egyptian origin of the Danaans is also attested by Hesiod,[30] and the importance of this clan—already Greek for some ten generations at the time of the Trojan War—is demonstrated by the fact that Homer calls the Greeks 'Achaeans' or 'Danaans' indifferently, according to whether he needs a short or a long syllable in any particular line.

Perseus married Andromeda, and had by her a son called Sthenelus, who succeeded him. Sthenelus married Nicippe, the daughter of Pelops, who had two brothers, Atreus and Thyestes. On the death of Sthenelus, Eurystheus ascended the throne of Mycenae.[31] He was a contemporary of Heracles, whom Herodotus dates to the period *circa* 1300,[32] and also imposed the traditional Twelve Labours on him.

We know that Eurystheus was born only a few days before Heracles,[33] and that the latter had a twin brother called Iphicles. As we shall see below, one of the most important political events in Bronze Age Greece was the violent death of Eurystheus during a Mycenean campaign in Attica. The man who actually killed the Danaan monarch was Iolaus, the son of Heracles' twin brother Iphicles. As the latter was born more or less simultaneously with Eurystheus, and since Iphicles could hardly have begotten Iolaus before the age of seventeen or eighteen: since, moreover, Iolaus himself must have attained a like age before he could take part in the campaign against the Mycenaeans in Attica, it therefore follows that Eurystheus cannot have been less than thirty-five years old at the time of his death.

Heracles' mother, Alcmene, had conceived her twins after intercourse with two different lovers: Heracles was begotten by Zeus, while Amphitryon sired Iphicles. As I have already mentioned, Iphicles' son Iolaus killed Eurystheus in Attica. Heracles had, by Deianeira, a son called Hyllus, who was destined to play an important part in history: it was he who attempted to lead the Heraclidae into the Peloponnese, probably after the capture of Thebes by the Epigoni in 1250. The expedition failed, and Hyllus was killed at the Isthmus by Echemus the Tegean. This abortive invasion must without doubt be connected with the Mycenean wall, also on the Isthmus, and certainly built not long before this event[34]—probably just prior to the campaign of the Seven against Thebes, *c.* 1275, as we shall see below.

The violent death of Eurystheus provoked a revolution at Mycenae: the Danaan-Perseïd house was ousted in favour of the Pelopidae, as represented by Atreus, who was one of Nicippe's blood-brothers, and thus the uncle of the murdered king. This revolution was accompanied by a great fire, which probably destroyed the palace of Perseus, and must be dated to the year 1285 or thereabouts.[35]

Atreus was, beyond any doubt, a very great sovereign. He rebuilt the palace and enlarged the ring-wall, shifting the western ramparts of the citadel in such a way as to both extend the perimeter and bring Schliemann's Grave Circle A within it. It was he, in all probability, who erected the famous Lion Gate and built the family tomb known today as the 'Treasury of Atreus'.[36] It was during his reign, and before the undertaking of the first, unsuccessful, expedition against Thebes, that the Achaeans accomplished the formidable task of buiding a wall right across the Isthmus.

Atreus was succeeded by his brother Thyestes, who must already have been well advanced in years when he came to the throne, and probably had a short reign. After him we are confronted with Atreus's son Agamemnon. This is the period of the Trojan War; so Agamemnon's reign must have ended in 1240. He was succeeded by the famous partnership of Clytemnestra and Aegisthus.

Orestes, too, must have been an important and capable ruler. It was he who built the third ring-wall of the citadel: I shall analyse the nature of this wall in greater detail below. He also succeeded to the throne of his paternal uncle Menelaus, and must have ruled over a large part of the Peloponnese, including Laconia.[37] His death took place shortly after 1200, and appears to have been the occasion for fresh disturbances: the buildings outside the citadel were burnt during this period—which also saw the destruction of Pylos. I shall discuss all these events in more detail in the appropriate place.

Orestes was succeeded by his son Tisamenes, who reigned until *c.* 1160, the date at which Mycenae was burnt by the people traditionally known as the Dorians. From this time on the city fell into complete oblivion.

By taking all these various complex factors into account, we arrive at the chronological table on p. 10, which leaves very little margin for variation in its dates. To particularise: Thyestes, even if we assume him to have been the youngest brother, cannot have reigned more than

MYCENAE

1405 The Palace of Cnossos burnt down by Achaean Invaders (first fire)

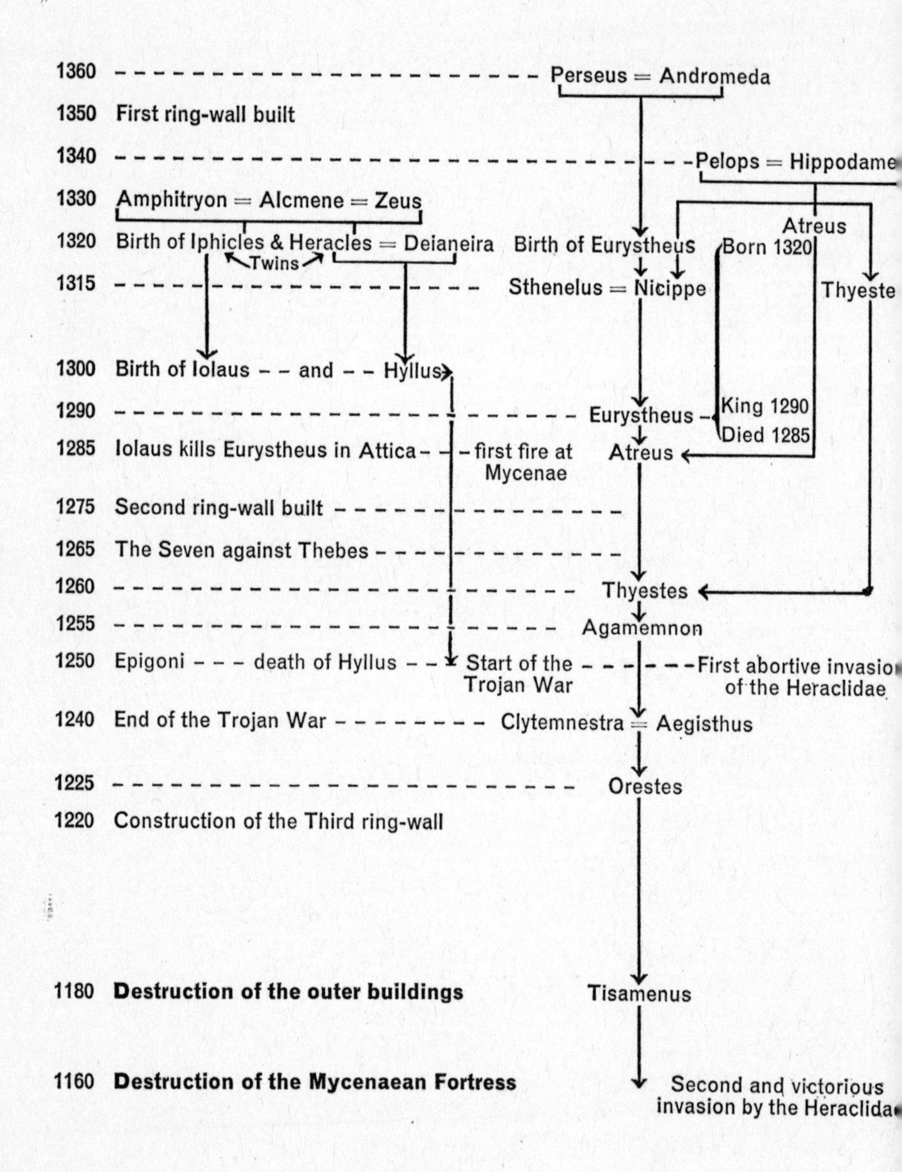

1100 Cnossos burnt for the second time

fifty years later than the marriage of his sister Nicippe: and, as I have already demonstrated, Eurystheus cannot have been killed before he was thirty-five. We must assume long reigns for Perseus, Atreus and Orestes: otherwise they could hardly have accomplished the various public works attributed to them.

The proposed date-scheme is also in harmony with the story, reported by Herodotus,[38] that after the death of Hyllus the Heraclidae swore to make no further incursions for a century. This oath probably reflects, in mythical terms, the historical fact that between 1250 and 1160 the Heraclidae made no attempt to regain the Peloponnese.

But what most encourages one's belief that the chronological table here set out might come very close to the historical sequence of events embodied in the myths is this. It so happens that, through the assassination of Eurystheus, the abortive campaign of the Seven against Thebes, and the victorious expedition of the Epigoni (which provoked the Heraclidae's attempt, under Hyllus's leadership, to invade the Peloponnese), the respective histories of the Mycenean dynasties and the Cadmean dynasty in Thebes are closely interrelated. Further, the chronological scheme advanced here is perfectly consistent with every factor needed to explain the great Boeotian city's tragic history. In fact, though Amphitryon and Alcmene were from Tiryns, they were domiciled in Thebes[39] when Heracles and Iphicles were born—both of whom, as I have already mentioned, were one day to play a preponderant role in Mycenean history.

But the Theban legend is, in its turn, indissolubly bound up with that of Crete, which covers a period anterior to the myths associated with Cadmus. This is why, before trying to reconstruct the history of the period in the subsequent chapters of my book, I shall now set out my second chronological scheme, based this time on the Cretan dynasty.

As I have said, I accept Palmer's chronology for Late Minoan III, and thus for Late Helladic III also; I further accept the theory that the first conquest of Cnossos by the Achaeans took place *c.* 1405. As I also mentioned above, the hypothesis of an early Greek dynasty corresponding to the 'Palace Style' period, between 1450 and 1400—this dynasty being supposedly overthrown by a local revolution[40]—cannot be maintained: this will become apparent when the point is discussed in detail in the following chapter.

Having secured a superb base for operations in Crete, the Achaeans, after first rebuilding the palaces[41] for their own use, proceeded to cast their eyes further afield. The first Achaean king of the island (legendary tradition gives him the name of Taurus, or Bull, and equates him with Zeus) made an expedition to Tyre, which, in the absence of the local ruler, Agenor,[42] he captured, carrying off Europa,[43] daughter of Phoenix, the eponymous first Phoenician. He built the mighty city of Gortyn for her in Crete, and there she gave birth to the first Minos.[44]

On his return King Agenor, determined to revenge himself for the injury he had suffered, sent off a powerful expeditionary force under the command of his son Cadmus,[45] with orders to bring Europa back again.[46] I shall have more to say at a later point about this extraordinary expedition, which in fact never reached its destination. Europa remained in Crete, and Gortyn was fortified[47]—the only city of the many on that great island to be so—perhaps as a precaution against possible reprisals by Agenor. Yet Cadmus's task force changed the whole course of late Bronze Age history, and thus probably left its mark on the subsequent history of Western Europe, down to our own times.

Let us now return to the Cretan dynasty for a little, and try to establish an approximate date-scheme for it. The first Minos was succeeded by his brother Rhadamanthus—his younger brother, in all probability. But Minos had a son, Deucalion, who does not appear to have reigned; Rhadamanthus was succeeded by Idomeneus, Deucalion's son and thus the grandson of Minos. Homer[48] tells us that Idomeneus already had white hair when he took part in the expedition against Troy.

We may note, lastly, that Taurus-Zeus had by Europa, in addition to Minos and Rhadamanthus, a third son called Sarpedon, who played a curious and isolated role in the history of this period. Again, I shall discuss Sarpedon's position more fully later.[49]

If we date the end of the Trojan War *c.* 1240, and assume that Idomeneus was then about sixty, it is reasonable to place the birth of his grandfather Minos at *c.* 1350, that of Rhadamanthus ten years later, and the raid on Tyre organised by Taurus-Zeus at approximately 1360, Taurus himself having been born round about 1380. We thus arrive at the chronological table on p. 13, which shows not only the putative dates of these rulers' births, but also the periods during which they may be presumed to have reigned. Rhadamanthus's reign is probably to be explained by the fact that Deucalion[50] was too young at the time of his father Minos's death (no more than ten according to the date-scheme) to succeed him on the throne. We must also presume that Deucalion died young (at twenty, according to the date-scheme) and before his uncle Rhadamanthus (who, I have calculated, lived to the age of sixty), thus leaving his son Idomeneus as heir to the throne, which he

CRETE

1405 **Palace of Cnossos burnt down by Achaean Invaders (first fire)**

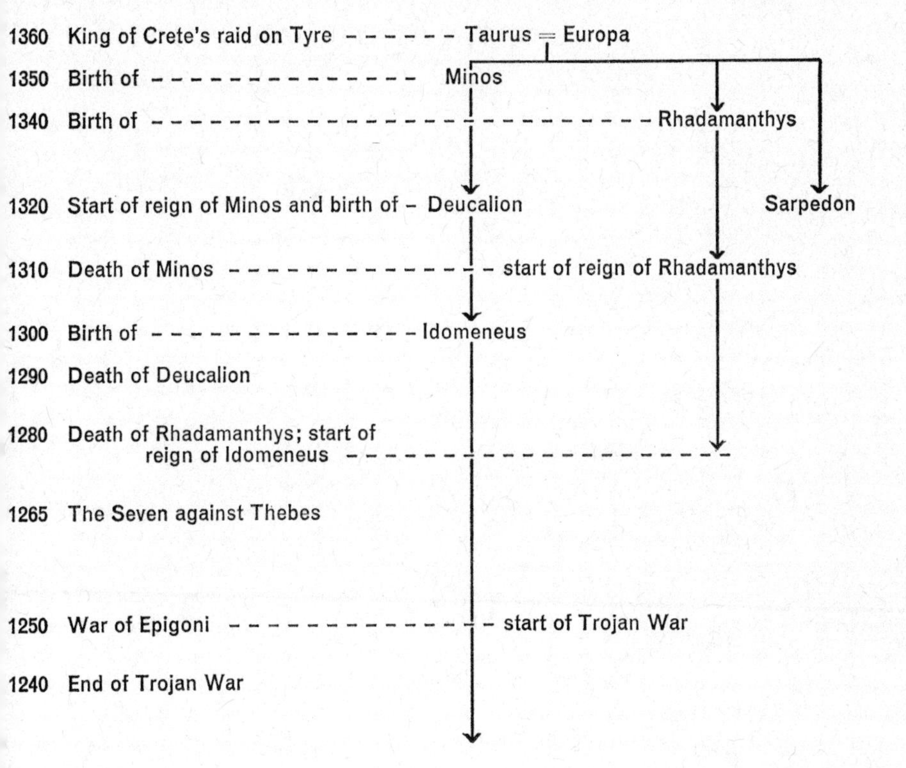

1180 **Destruction of Pylos**

1160 **Destruction of Mycenae**

1100 **Cnossos burnt for the second time**

ascended on the death of his uncle. These various requirements, again, leave an extremely small margin for altering any date in the proposed scheme.

The scheme itself I consider fairly satisfactory, especially since by placing Taurus's raid on Tyre roughly at 1360, it makes Taurus a near-contemporary of Perseus—who was also born of a nymph and a god. It is beginning to become clear that the first quarter of the fourteenth century B.C. represents the furthest limit at which we can extract any genuine historical substratum from the Greek myths. The Greeks had, of course, been established in Greece long before that date; but in the present state of our knowledge it remains impossible to go back any further, except perhaps for one or two isolated facts which can be established and dated by archaeological methods.

It was, then, about 1360, or perhaps a little earlier, that Cadmus's famous punitive expedition was launched by Agenor, King of Tyre. Cadmus must have been a man of extraordinary genius, with a quite exceptional gift for organisation; but he never reached Crete. He put in at Thera,[51] after which we find him at Delphi and, finally, in Thebes. There is nothing odd about his first port of call: this was a period when sailors always tried to avoid long voyages across open sea, and confined themselves, as far as possible, to coastal navigation. Cadmus's fleet might well have hugged the Asiatic coast as far as the neighbourhood of Miletus. But his subsequent itinerary requires some explanation. The men of Tyre were renowned as sailors, and can hardly have made so gross a navigational error; besides, at this period it was almost impossible to travel from Thera to Delphi by sea, especially if one did not have friendly ports and revictualling points along one's route. I shall return at greater length to this crucial episode in Greek Bronze Age history when discussing the myths of Aristeus and of Cadmus's daughter Autonoë.

First, however, we must attempt to establish a date-scheme for the Cadmean dynasty. This dynasty was, beyond any possible doubt, founded by Cadmus in Thebes about the middle of the fourteenth century B.C. Here, too, was the site of the famous fortress known as the Cadmeia.

For the chronology of Cadmos, the last excavations by Dr N. Platon at Thebes have confirmed the chronology that I had suggested in the French edition of the present book. Dr Platon has found in the Cadmeia a collection of Babylonian cylinders of 'which at least two have the appearance of genuine imported pieces from Babylonia, and one

1 A Babylonian cylinder seal (enlarged) found at Thebes

2a Weapons used for ceremonial purposes only

b Mycenaean charioteer stele

of them by a most fortunate chance bears an inscription which can be dated with precision. Its design shows a bearded deity emerging from between two mountain peaks; he holds aloft two inverted vessels, from which streams of water flow down into two similar vessels standing on the ground. He is evidently the weather god dispensing rain. The mountain peaks are each crowned with a flower-like object presumably intended to represent a tree, and similar "trees" stand at their bases. The space between the mountains and the streams of water is filled on either side by flowers or rosettes.

'The inscription on this seal reads: "Kidin-Marduk, son of Sha-ili-madamqa, officer of Burraburiash, King of the World". This is the name of the owner of the seal, and it is interesting that another seal of this same official is at present in the Berlin Museum. The designs on the two seals are totally different and the inscriptions, though similar, are not identical, for the Berlin seal has an extra line of writing and a quite different disposition of the signs.

'Now Burraburiash was the name of at least two, possibly three, kings of the Third (Kassite) Dynasty of Babylon; but only the last can be considered as the king whose name appears on this seal, since only he laid claim to the title "King of the World" (*Šar kiššati*). This Burraburiash indeed is one of the best-known figures of the "Amarna Age", for he is the author of six of the famous Tell el-Amarna letters. He ruled for twenty-eight years, roughly from 1381 to 1354 B.C. Thus the seal could not have been made before 1381 B.C.

'Moreover, it could only have started on its travels after the death of its owner, Kidin-Marduk, when it had ceased to perform its primary function as a personal signet and could pass freely from hand to hand as a valuable talisman. It is of course impossible to say how long it might take for such an object to find its way, by trade or diplomatic mission, from its place of origin to such a distant foreign capital, or how long it remained there before being abandoned where it was found. But it is clear that it could hardly have reached its final resting-place before about 1375 B.C., even if Kidin-Marduk died in office and was appointed at the very beginning of the reign, and these are unwarranted assumptions. The date of its deposit is likely to be considerably—perhaps many decades—later than this.

'It is a remarkable fact that up till now only eleven imported cylinder seals have been found in the Aegean area, and only two of these—both found in Crete—are certainly from Babylon itself. Even if the reported presence of unfinished or even blank seals should prove that the hoard is partly the work of an ancient Theban imitator of Babylonian products, it would still be necessary to assume that he had the originals before him and so the chronological value of the find would be unimpaired.'[52]

It seems therefore very probable that Cadmus brought with him the original seals from Tyre as talismans and a date around 1360 would appear the most likely for the voyage of Cadmus and the importation of the amulets.

But these cylinders inscribed in cuneiform script likewise give, in all probability, the necessary clue for our understanding of the controversial and much discussed passage in Herodotus,[53] in which he attributes to the companions of Cadmus the introduction of the first letters into Greece. The three tripods shown to Herodotus and inscribed with characters 'resembling the Ionian script' can naturally not have dated back to the days of Cadmus. The Phoenician script was not in use in Greece before the eighth century and did not exist in the fourteenth; furthermore the dialect used in the inscriptions, as transcribed by Herodotus, is very much later than the Achaean dialect of the B tablets. But on the other hand it might seem reasonable to believe that the first generation of the Tyrian immigrants who came with Cadmus could read and write the cuneiform script, and this may well be the origin of the tradition mentioned by Herodotus. Two centuries later the inhabitants of Thebes were using the Linear B script for writing Greek.[54]

Cadmus had married Harmonia, the daughter of Aphrodite; by her he had several children, whose subsequent history we will consider later. In particular she bore him a son called Polydorus, who succeeded him.[55] Polydorus in turn begot Labdacus, who ascended the throne in his stead,[56] and Labdacus in turn begot Laïus as his son and heir. Laïus, who was thus the great-grandson of Cadmus,[57] died at the hands of his own son, Oedipus; Oedipus married his own mother, Jocasta, and had two sons by her, Eteocles and Polynices. These two princes died young, at each other's hand, during the war of the Seven against Thebes—that is, about 1265 according to the chronology we have already established. The direct Cadmean line thus became extinct, and the crown reverted to Jocasta's brother, Creon, whose son Maniceus had likewise died in battle. Creon's reign probably lasted until the war of the Epigoni (i.e. till 1250), when Thebes fell and her sovereigns vanished from history.

We may note that Laïus's reign must have lasted about twenty years for Oedipus to attain an age at which he could kill him and after-

THEBES

1405 Palace of Cnossos burnt down by Achaean Invaders (first fire)

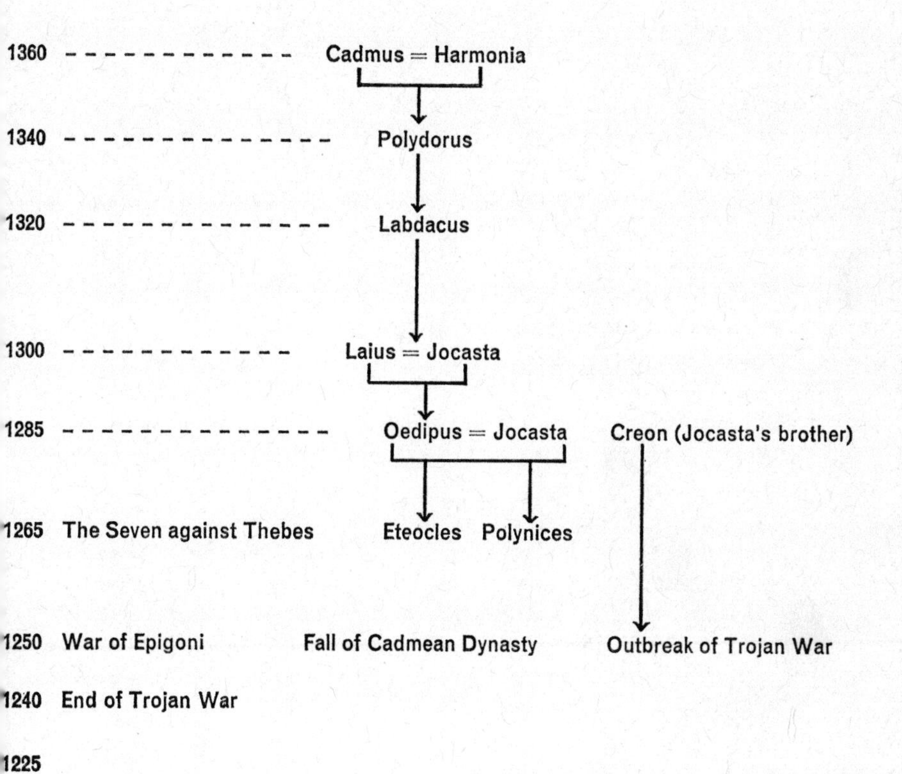

1180 Destruction of Pylos

1160 Destruction of Mycenae

100 Second burning of Cnossos

wards marry Jocasta. Oedipus's own reign must have likewise lasted about twenty years for his two sons to be able to take part, and kill each other, in the war of the Seven against Thebes. Though Oedipus himself could have been born some years before Laïus ascended the Theban throne, the same cannot be said of Eteocles and Polynices, who, obviously, were born after Oedipus's accession and his union with Jocasta.

Taking all these factors into account, we reach something like the genealogical tree on p. 17. The date-scheme suggests that if Creon was thirty at the time when Oedipus became king, he must himself have reigned till the age of sixty-five in order to perish in the War of the Epigoni. This does not seem excessive.

If we now combine these three chronological tables into one, so as to compare them more easily—see p. 18a—the historical pattern of the Greek world at the close of the Bronze Age, during the periods known as Late Helladic III and Late Minoan III, becomes clearly visible. Starting from a mythical epoch that ends shortly before the Achaean invasion of Crete in 1405, we can observe the main events associated with the Bronze Age. The war of the Seven against Thebes, the war of the Epigoni or Successors, the Trojan war and the return of the Heraclidae—these in a sense shape the destiny of the various royal houses during our period. We can trace the dynasties of Thebes and Mycenae to the moment of their final extinction. For Crete, unfortunately, we possess no evidence after the death of Idomeneus. The Linear B tablets from Cnossos, baked hard by a second palace fire *c.* 1100, do indeed mention a local sovereign, but only refer to him by his title of *wanax*, or 'king'. In the present state of the evidence it seems unlikely that we can squeeze any more conclusions from our sources, whether literary, mythical, or archaeological. We can only hope that fresh discoveries will one day enable us to fill the gap in our knowledge of the Cretan dynasty between 1230 and *c.* 1100, and to learn just who these *wanak[t]es* were.

We may also note that this chronological chart confirms the testimony of Thucydides,[58] according to whom the Dorians and the Heraclidae occupied the Peloponnese eighty years after the fall of Troy. Finally, it is worth emphasising that the correlation of the individual three date-schemes makes it still more difficult to alter a date in any one of them without producing several palpable absurdities in another. The various events have become, as they should be, interdependent.[59] For this reason I regard my chronological scheme as being more or less accurate, and in any case adequate for an interpretation of the human motives which drove these highly civilised men to act as they did.

The rest of this book is an attempt to reconstruct their history as plausibly as possible: I have utilised all the knowledge at our disposal, whether in the social, religious, or economic field, in an effort to understand the men who lived through this period—those far-off ancestors of ours to whom we owe Homeric poetry, and the Linear B tablets, and the splendours of Mycenean art.

CHAPTER II

The Period Before 1400

It is not my intention to examine the complex problems posed by an analysis of tribal movements during the Early and Middle Helladic periods. The subject is still highly controversial, and I shall do no more here than attempt to establish and recapitulate such facts as may have a bearing on my main theme.

The Early Helladic period has left us the extraordinary Palace of Lerna[60] (to the foot of which Heracles must have come to kill the Hydra at Eurystheus's bidding), and the remains of various settlements, scattered as far afield as Thessaly. This was a neolithic culture: we find frequent instances of pots made without the wheel, and tools fashioned from stone or bone—though it is not impossible that some of these tribes may have been familiar with copper. The palatial buildings they erected are all the more amazing when one considers how early and primitive a people they were.

The first Greek-speaking tribes seem to have appeared in Greece itself during the Middle Bronze Age (Middle Helladic), that is, somewhere between 1900 and 1600. Tradition places them at the beginning of this period, though today some scholars argue for their having arrived about 1600.[61] If one adopts the second of these hypotheses, it follows that the first waves of immigrants must have come into immediate contact with the contemporary civilisation of Crete; if, on the other hand, one chooses the first theory, the early immigrants would have been settled in the country for several hundred years before this vitally important contact was established.[62]

The first hypothesis seems barely tenable, but the second contains numerous difficulties which have not yet been resolved. If we connect the Luwians of Asia Minor with grey Minyan ware,[63] it is tempting to suppose that they arrived before the Greeks, after founding Troy. This would resolve[64] the knotty problem of those countless Greek geographical names—Parnassus, Tiryns, and so on—which are of non-Greek origin. The existence of early Minyan ware at Beycesultan,[65] where a bull-cult was practised, may very well indicate the date of the Luwian invasion of Greece—or at least a period immediately preceding it.[66]

Whatever the truth as regards mainland Greece, it appears certain that the Luwians were established in Crete, and are to be identified with the 'Minoans' of antiquity. But various major difficulties arise at this point. Only one single sherd of grey Minyan ware—and that undoubtedly an import—has been discovered in Crete;[67] nor is there any Minyan pottery among the sherds (dating back to the Bronze Age) which have turned up at Delphi,[68] where the Luwians are supposed to have had their principal temple, PARNA-ASSOS. If Minyan ware is taken as being the distinctive mark of the Luwians, this double blank is curious, to say the least of it.

However, the absence of Minyan ware in Crete and at Delphi is not a decisive argument for the rejection of the Luwian hypothesis, and our interpretation must pay due regard to the linguistic no less than the archaeological evidence. On p. 22 I have sketched out, in diagrammatic form, a concise account of the sequence of pottery-styles in Crete, as I conceive them to have been. The most important single fact is that the Luwian invasion of 1700, far from marking a cultural break, was, on the contrary, the immediate prelude to the island's highest peak of artistic achievement and that the existing inhabitants made no attempt whatsoever to resist these newcomers in any respect. These facts, it seems to me, are capable of one interpretation only. The first wave of invaders (who arrived *c.* 2200) was also Luwian in origin: bearing in mind the early date at which they appeared, it may be assumed that they had not yet learnt how to manufacture Minyan ware, and employed neolithic potting techniques. But when the second wave of Luwian invaders reached Crete, five hundred years later, local craftsmen were producing such superb pottery that the newcomers abandoned their own Minyan style altogether.[69]

Another point: in the Homeric Hymn concerning him, Apollo commands some Minoan sailors from Cnossos to go and found a cult-centre in his honour at Crisa, below Mount Parnassus.[70] Now Apollo had put to sea with his Cretan followers; he had the form of a sacred dolphin, and *delphinios* was one of his special epithets. Nor was this all: Crisa possessed deposits of tin, the importance of which could hardly be exaggerated in a civilisation based on bronze. In the eastern Mediterranean copper is relatively plentiful, but tin very rare. To deify the uncommon is a very human trait, and to place the mine under the God's

CHRONOLOGY OF CRETAN POTTERY

(The dates indicate the first appearance of each style)

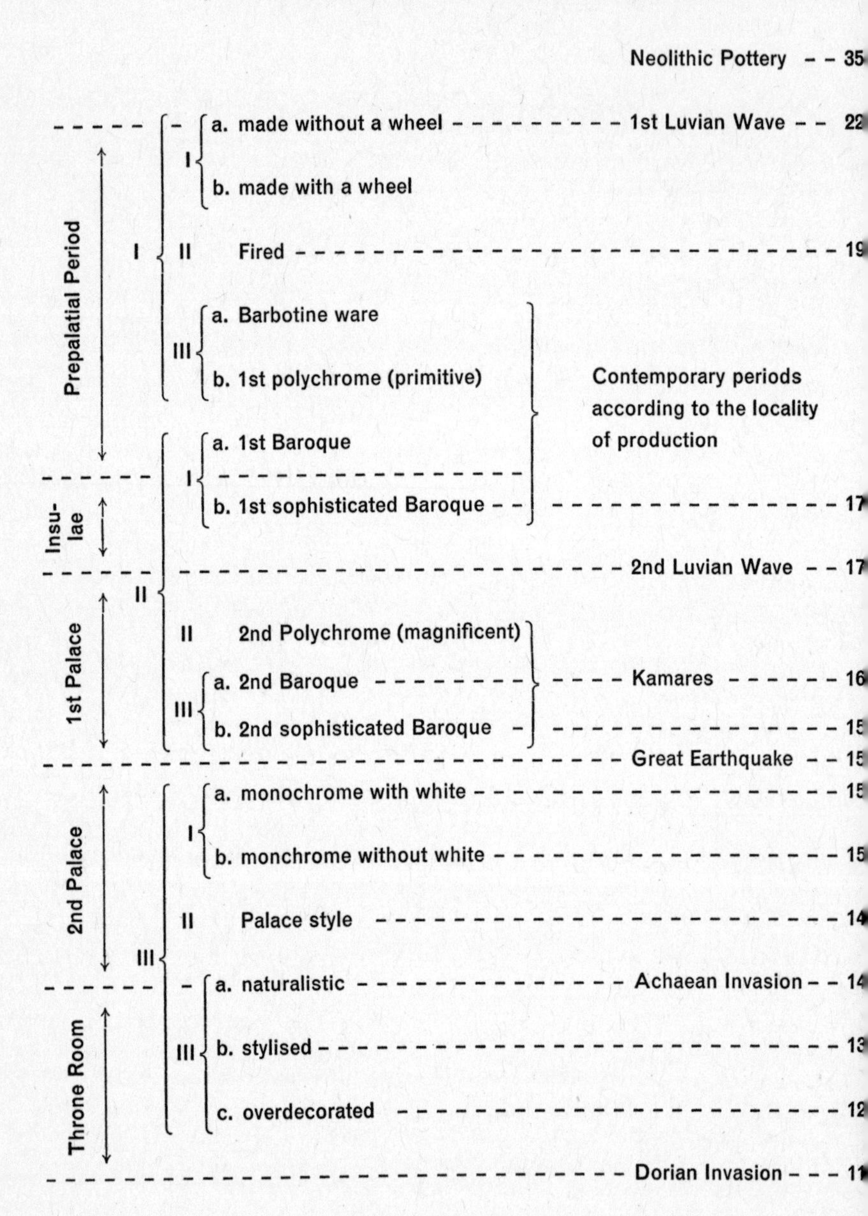

protection was perhaps a kind of insurance policy. Parna-Assos, in Luwian, means 'the place of the temple', and there cannot be the slightest doubt that Parnassus is the name of a Luwian cult-centre.

Now there was a Corcyraean grotto on Mount Parnassus, and another in Cilicia, where the Luwians had settled not later than the middle of the second millennium B.C. From all this we may infer that the priests who established the cult of Apollo Delphinios at the foot of Parnassus were Luwians: a very powerful argument in favour of the hypothesis that Luwians were also settled in Crete during the second millennium B.C.,[71] and a satisfying explanation of those Cretan geographical names with a -sos termination, such as Cnossos or Amnisos. However, it should be emphasised that the total absence of Minyan ware, both in Crete and at Delphi, obliges us to suppose that these Luwians reached Crete before the era in which it was produced—i.e. about 2200 B.C.[72]

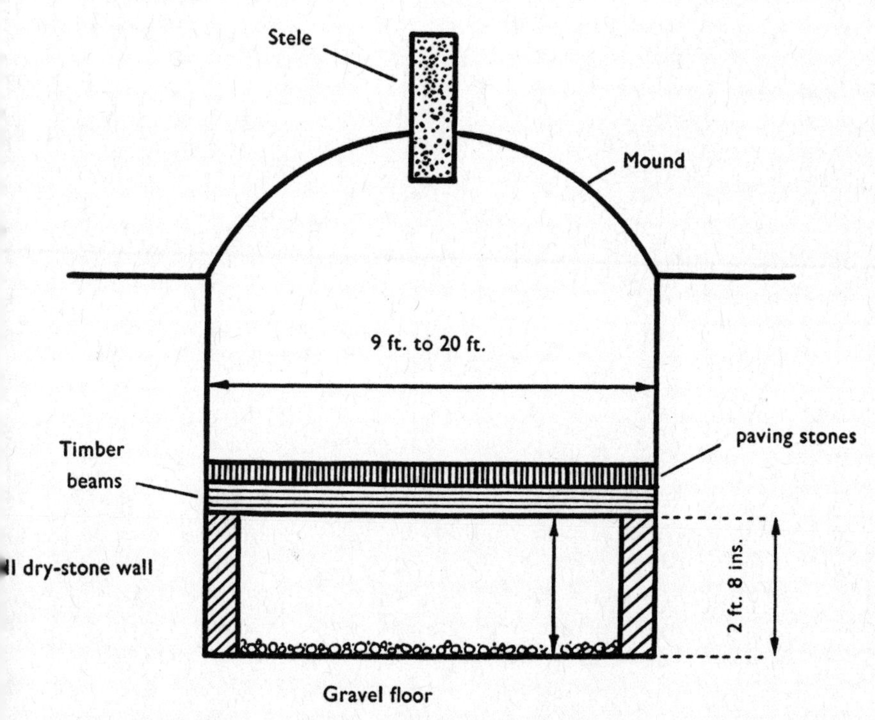

Diagram showing a shaft tomb in cross-section

Those who oppose the theory of an early Indo-European invasion *c.* 1900 rest their case largely on the continuity of burial customs in mainland Greece. It is not true, they say, that the Greeks only appeared on the scene in 1600, bringing the horse with them. Every intermediate form of inhumation can be shown to exist, from the individual urn-burial containing one crouching body to the beehive-shaped family vaults that existed at the close of the Bronze Age,[73] not to mention shaft-graves and tombs carved from the solid rock.

But is it logical to argue, from this continuity, that no other immigrants can have arrived during the period? Not all scholars think so.[74] In any case such uniformity or divergence of burial customs must be studied in connection with the religious beliefs behind them. When a group of Christians emigrates to another Christian country, we can hardly hope to deduce their nationality from their burial customs: they share the same religious beliefs, though one group may be Irish and the other Italian. But in the same social context a Jewish cemetery would be distinguishable at a glance. If invaders and invaded professed the same religion, the invasion can have left no tell-tale marks on either side's burial customs.

Now we know that both Luwians and Achaeans adored a Bull-God: in other words, that they had deified the animal on which they lived, and besought the resultant divinity to accomplish the mysterious annual ritual of fertility on their behalf.[75] Horns of consecration, bulls' horns, turn up everywhere: we find them on altars, temples, house-gables. This practice is not confined to mainland Greece, still less to Crete; it is common throughout the East amongst peoples whose pastoral economy has for centuries depended on the bull.[76] So the absence of any obvious 'break' merely shows that there was no change of cult; it tells us nothing about the cult's practitioners.

Furthermore, even if Greek burial customs during the Middle and Late Helladic periods do display a continuous pattern of evolution, there can be little doubt that this evolution is remarkably radical, beginning with jars and culminating in the ashlar jointed *tholos* tomb. (It is obvious that various types of burial existed during the same period. There was no authority to prescribe or forbid them, and not everyone could afford a *tholos* tomb, or even a shaft-grave.) The evidence does not suggest that a civilisation, when left to itself, develops in so radical a fashion. The Danaans might well have imported the Egyptian notion of the rock-tomb, and the *tholos* was very probably due, as we shall see, to the building of the second temple at Delphi.

But *who* was it reacted against the practice of burying the dead, packed like so many foetuses, in individual jars, and moved towards a form of collective burial where skeletons, once the flesh had rotted off them, were treated as mere trash? If we have only a single race to deal with, the human problem is not an easy one. If, on the other hand, we are concerned with two different races, possessing a common religion but divergent ritually, then the one can influence the other without catastrophic results. In any case the spontaneous evolution of a custom to a point where it becomes totally self-contradictory is a quite unknown human phenomenon; and from an interpretation of the archaeological evidence it would appear that we have two separate sources reacting on one another, not a single civilisation endowed with some strange capacity for self-development unknown in other fields. This is all the more likely when we remember that religion tends to be the most conservative of all social phenomena.[77]

There are two other very important points which support the notion of a double invasion. The chronological scheme for Mycenean pottery established by Furumark[78] does not go back beyond 1550, and a highly pertinent explanation must be found for this fact if there was only one wave of invaders. Now the mythical and literary tradition preserved by Hesiod distinguishes clearly between two separate invasions of the

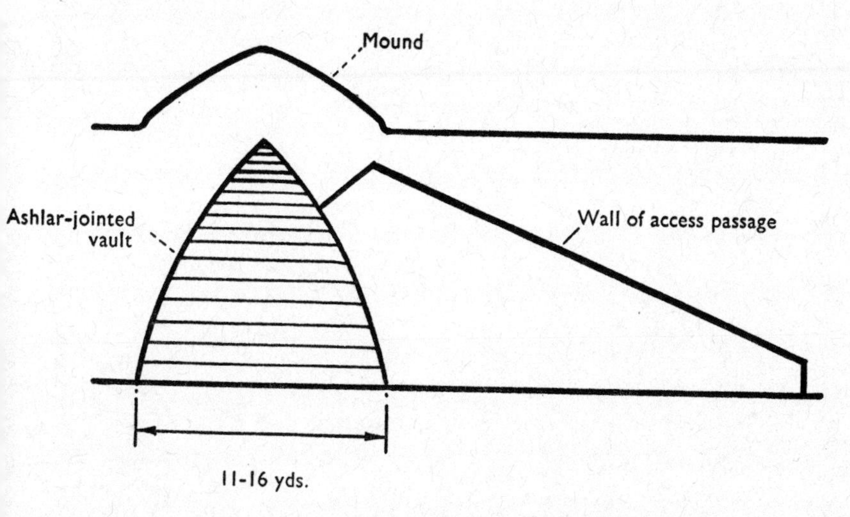

Diagram of a beehive tomb in cross-section

Greek peninsula. The men of the Bronze Age disappeared, and were replaced by a race that was 'better and nobler, the wonderful generation of hero-men, who are also called half-gods, the generation before our own on this vast earth'.[79] There could be no plainer reference to the first Greeks, who, the poet specifies, took part in the war against seven-gated Thebes and the expedition to Troy. For a century now we have seen, again and again, how often the ancient Greek tradition contains historical truth, and it would require very cogent arguments to refute Hesiod here.

Before we embark on the history of the Achaeans one further point deserves some consideration, and that is the history of their language, which has been preserved for us on a series of clay tablets, baked hard when the palaces were destroyed by fire. These tablets are the annual inventory of Crown property, and we know them today as the Linear B tablets: they replace earlier tablets known as Linear A, which were previously employed in Crete. These Linear A tablets have been found almost everywhere on the island; examples of Linear B have turned up at Cnossos, Pylos, Mycenae and Thebes. We also possess objects bearing inscriptions in both A and B.[80] Both systems of writing are syllabic, and B's characters are obviously derived from A. We cannot read A, and it seems unlikely that we ever shall, since there are not enough examples of the script in existence to work on statistically[81]—as Ventris did with B, proving ultimately that the language they used was Greek. But is the text of the Linear B tablets *exclusively* Greek, or do they perhaps employ a dialect compound of Greek and words borrowed from some other language?[82]

One immediately striking characteristic of Linear B is its resistance to change. The Pylos tablets predate those from Cnossos by nearly a century.[83] The Greek on the Cnossos tablets, moreover, is slightly more developed than that on the Pylos ones. But whatever the solution one adopts, it remains quite incredible that the Pylos tablets were written by non-Greek scribes. The first scribes who, about 1400 B.C., transformed the A script of Cnossos into a B script capable of reproducing Greek *may*—in Crete, at any rate—have been bilingual Minoans. But that the scribes on the mainland, at Pylos and Mycenae, should still be Minoans six generations later—this is a supposition which defies all the laws of probability. If the mainland tablets from a period about 1200 contain words of non-Greek origin, we cannot attribute their appearance to the scribes' ignorance of the language their masters spoke: two centuries of assimilation exclude such a possibility.

a	e	i	o	u	a_2(ha)
da	de	di	do	du	ai
ja	je		jo		ai_2 ?
ka	ke	ki	ko	ku	ai_3 ?
ma	me	mi	mo	mu	kwe ?
na	ne	ni	no	nu	mwa
pa	pe	pi	po	pu	pa_2
	qe	qi	qo		pa_3 ?
ra	re	ri	ro	ru	pte
sa	se	si	so	su	pu_2
ta	te	ti	to	tu	ra_2 ri-ja
wa	we	wi	wo		ra_3 rai
za	ze		zo	zu	ro_2 rijo

The principal characters of the Linear B Script*

As I have said, all the tablets in our possession consist of inventories, and are therefore necessarily repetitive to a degree in their vocabulary. A total of 3,500 tablets has yielded a total of 990 words—excluding proper names, which comprise nearly 65 per cent of the textual matter. Of these 990 words, 260 are no more than variants of spelling or dialect. Out of the 630 that are left, only 252 (according to the decipherers themselves[84]) possess a true Homeric equivalent or survive in some classical form, and bear a direct, linguistically convincing relationship to the context in which they are found. But a fair proportion even of these words consists of adjectives derived from nouns, such as *a-ko-ra*

*See Appendix 2

and *a-ko-ra-jo* (Greek *agorâ* and *agoraîos*) or *da-mo* and *da-mi-jo* (*dâmos* and *dâmios*). We can find thirty-five such doublets. We might find something like a dozen more words derived from proper names, and Palmer has added some thirty more plausible words in his last work.[85]

We are finally left with about 250 or 260 Greek words against 370 that cannot be identified at all. Nor is it any good blaming the vagaries of Mycenean spelling conventions; here they operate in favour of the possibility of identifying a word with its Greek equivalent. 260 against 630 means rather less than one word in two.[86] This is a very low proportion, even when we allow for the antiquity of the tablets; and the idea that they may be written in a mixture of Greek and non-Greek[87] has perhaps been rejected a little too hastily in the enthusiasm that greeted that first victory over silence and the unknown.[88]

The hypothesis of a bilingual dialect seems particularly tempting because the Achaeans in Crete must surely have been in close contact with the Minoans—that is, with the people whom today we know as the Luwians. So if the Linear B tablets found at Cnossos contain any non-Greek words, there is every likelihood of these words having a Luwian provenance; and since the tablets found in Crete and mainland Greece both write the same language and employ the same characters, we have strong support for the hypothesis of an initial Luwian invasion, followed *c.* 1600 by a peaceful merging with the Achaeans, who brought with them not only the bull but also the horse.

The introduction of the horse by the Achaeans might explain why the Luwians on the mainland did not maintain contact with their Cretan cousins. The dispersion area of Minyan ware in mainland Greece shows how widely scattered the Luwian settlements were, from the southern Peloponnese to the north of Boeotia. The population was small, and without the aid of the horse communications would have been difficult in the extreme: a fact which might explain the relative stagnation of these settlements when we compare them with the far more densely populated centres on Crete. This is why true Mycenean pottery does not make its first appearance till after 1600.

As we shall see presently, the problem of Troy[89] is very similar to that of Mycenae, with one great difference: no inscribed tablets have been found in Troy, and because of this it remains, for the time being at least, a linguistic enigma.

Despite all this—and whatever may be the final solution which an increasingly stringent analysis produces in respect of the Luwian problem—we shall still find mainland Greece occupied, *c.* 1600 B.C., by a people who spoke some kind of Greek dialect. These folk lived in open villages, and were ignorant of fortifications—except, perhaps, for wooden palisades or unbaked brick walls, which left no traces of their existence after a few centuries. They almost certainly came from Asia Minor[90] and when they migrated they must have driven their herds in front of them: cattle, smaller livestock and horses. At this period agriculture was still in its infancy, and the migrant tribes naturally gravitated towards areas suitable for grazing the cattle on which their lives depended. The makers of Minyan and even proto-Minyan ware had already deified the bull: this was only natural in a period when man always wove his myths round those animals which gave him sustenance, and on which he relied so much.

These migrant groups, then, must have settled in the plains, and especially in those marshy plains suitable for the grazing of cattle. It is a constant feature of the Middle Bronze Age, when Greece was thinly populated and men could choose the region they preferred, that a herdsman's habitat tended to be dictated by the particular type of livestock he kept. Later, as we shall see, the population increase exactly reversed this trend, and it was the living-area forced on the herdsman which determined the kind of livestock he kept. When this happened, the myths woven round the foster-animal underwent a corresponding change. This new pastoral group developed a Goat-God which finally came into direct conflict with the Bull-God, so that war broke out between the respective followers of Zagreus and Dionysus. Religious wars are always the fiercest; and if we examine the evidence carefully we can always detect, behind some supernatural image, those social and economic conditions which gave rise to it. And when conditions reverse themselves, some men usually switch their allegiance, but there always remains a hard core of convinced fanatics. If we do not make allowance for this abstruse—but extremely human—factor, history in general, and most particularly Bronze Age history, is bound to remain meaningless for us.

But in 1600 problems of overpopulation did not yet exist, and there was no need for the harsh rationing system which the Linear B tablets reveal to us: there must have been enough space, and food, for everyone. We may also note that marshland makes ideal pasturage for horned cattle and horses: they never crop it barren. Today we still breed thousands of bulls and horses annually in the Camargue, and these herds remain more or less static. People who live by such herds therefore tend to make permanent settlements, colonising the shores of swampy

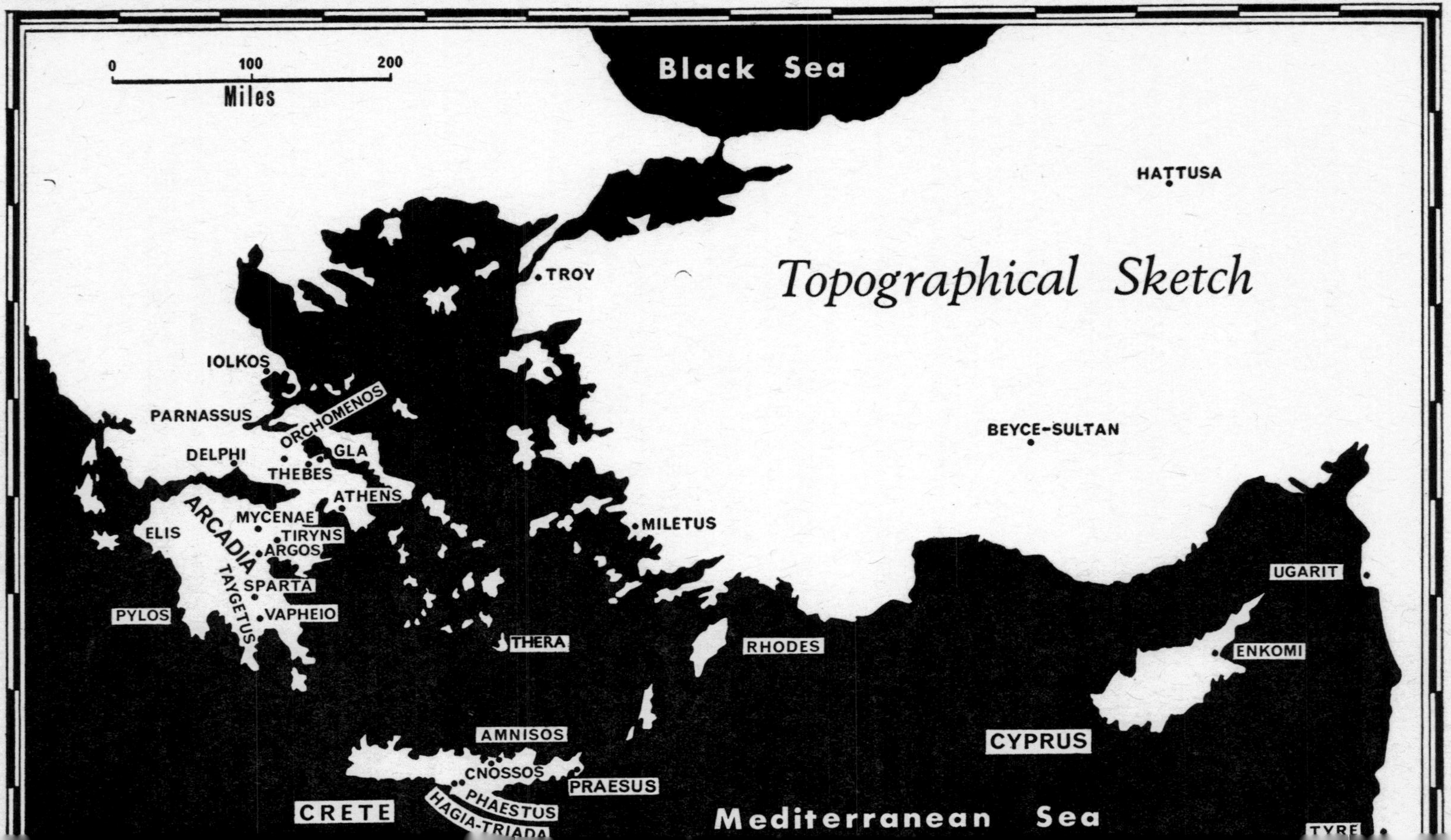

Topographical Sketch

0 100 200
Miles

Black Sea
HATTUSA
TROY
BEYCE-SULTAN
IOLKOS
PARNASSUS
ORCHOMENOS
DELPHI
GLA
THEBES
ATHENS
MYCENAE
ELIS
ARCADIA
TIRYNS
ARGOS
MILETUS
TAYGETUS
SPARTA
PYLOS
VAPHEIO
THERA
RHODES
UGARIT
ENKOMI
AMNISOS
CYPRUS
CNOSSOS
PRAESUS
PHAESTUS
HAGIA-TRIADA
CRETE
Mediterranean Sea
TYRE

lakes and the islands to be found in the middle of such lakes. This explains the vital importance of Lake Copaïs, that huge, marshy expanse in the heart of Boeotia, which gives so striking an emphasis to Homer's Catalogue of Ships. The marshy Argive plain likewise played an immensely important role in early Greek history; the swampland of Navarino was responsible for the existence of Pylos; and we know that on their march south to the Peloponnese the Achaeans founded a town in the humid coastal plain, on the site of modern Patras.[91] The same is true of Elis, which legend associates with that eponymous figure Pelops,[92] and, indeed, of the modern Tripolis plain, in the heart of mountainous Arcadia, where to this day Lake Taka guarantees a humid atmosphere—precious gift—all the year round.

But even the most superficial acquaintance with Greece makes it clear that such terrain, capable of supporting large cattle and horses indefinitely, forms only a tiny proportion (about 7 per cent) of the country's total area. Here, and nowhere else, permanent settlements based on stock-farming could take root, survive, and flourish. The small plains of Greece are not all that rich; but they are incomparably more fertile than the hill country, even the foothills, where soil can only be kept *in situ* by terracing.[93] When those who reared sheep or goats were driven up into the hills, they soon found themselves forced to lead the rough, semi-nomadic life which their descendants still lead today in many regions of Greece. This is particularly true of those who depend on goats for a living. The goat is most destructive in its habits, and soon exhausts any grazing-area, thus forcing the goatherds to move on in search of new pasturage. Through dint of constant enforced migrations, such peoples become, in the long run, tougher and more warlike than those who settle in the rich plains and get fat pickings there. Such factors had a considerable influence on the course of history until agriculture, to a very large extent, came to replace stock-farming as a means of livelihood. But at the time we are considering that point had not yet been reached.

It is an interesting fact that though the Greeks worshipped both the bull and the goat, they never displayed the same veneration for the ram, as Asiatic peoples did. Yet there must have been very considerable flocks of sheep in Greece. Penelope was always spinning wool, and the Cnossos tablets mention large numbers of such flocks, about which I shall have more to say presently. Though the point is not capable of final proof, it might perhaps be suggested that the shepherds, since they could neither go right into the mountains nor pasture their flocks in the plain, were forced—as is still the case today—to manage as best they could in the foothills and upland valleys.[94] They were thus always caught between the cattlemen of the plains and the mountain goatherds, and never achieved true independence.

One fact which seems symptomatic of such a situation is this: the Achaean rulers in Crete imposed no taxes on either the cattle or the horses of the nobles who inhabited the rich plainland, nor on the wandering goatherds, whose remote and rocky fastnesses placed them beyond reach of the central authority; but the shepherds were invariably made to pay up—though often, as we shall see, taxes of this sort fell far below the estimated figure, which shows that even dwellers in the foothills could, on occasion, defy a supposedly all-powerful government.[95]

Between 1600 and 1400 almost our sole evidence for the life of these pastoral clans stems from their burial-remains. We find their graves developing from the sunken cist-type[96] to the beehive *tholos*,[97] by way of rock-tombs which probably derived from the Egyptian style, and were brought to Greece by the Danaans in the first half of the sixteenth century B.C., at the time when the Hyksos were driven out of Egypt. I shall have occasion to expand on this point later, but I do not propose to give an account of Achaean burial customs, a task already carried out for us by the archaeologists.

I merely wish to note, apropos the subject with which I am primarily concerned, that the most original and most typically Greek aspect of Achaean burial customs consists in their habit of erecting sculptured or painted funerary *stelae*. This practice appears very early, long before the building of the palaces. Grave Circle B at Mycenae dates back at least to the last quarter of the seventeenth century B.C., and Grave Circle A to the following century. Both were quite certainly complete in 1450, and fell into disuse from then on. It may be apposite to note, at this juncture, the subject-matter of the two sculptured *stelae* found in Grave Circle B, and datable to *c.* 1600 B.C. One portrays a bull charging a shepherd, who was probably killed in such an accident, and must have been buried in the corresponding tomb (alpha); while the other shows us a shepherd defending a bull from the attack of a lion. As is common in primitive art, we have on a second level the representation of the dead bull and the dying lion. This shepherd must be among the four skeletons discovered in the tomb (gamma), which was an exceptionally rich one: from it came the only surviving portraits of Achaeans during this period, an electrum mask and an engraved amethyst.[98] The fact that these guardians of the herds were entitled to such sumptuous tombs says much for the importance of the role which livestock played in the economy of the period.

During the two centuries between 1600 and 1400, the populations of both Crete and mainland Greece appear to have lived in comparative peace amongst themselves. The best proof of this is the total absence of any fortification. The Cretans had suppressed piracy,[99] and their thalassocracy was at its height. The numerous references to piracy in the Homeric poems[100] prove that it was a common occurrence at the beginning of the Bronze Age. Thucydides' reference[101] to the suppression of Carian piracy by Minos clearly is concerned with sea-raiders of the Minoan period, whatever precise meaning we may attach to the names 'Minos' and 'Carian'. Clei[to]demus, as quoted by Plutarch,[102] even mentions a police action which Jason supposedly carried out.[103]

Both Cretans and Achaeans, being effectively isolated by the sea, reached great heights of prosperity during these two centuries. From about 1550 to 1400 the Cretans maintained an unbroken connection with Egypt, and are frequently mentioned in Pharaonic records. Their relations with the mainland likewise became progressively closer as time went on, and their influence on the style of Mycenean artifacts more obvious. Together with these developments came what can only be termed an internationalisation of Mycenean art.[104] After 1450 it is even possible that, where Cnossos itself was concerned, the stream of influence reversed its direction, and that some local sovereign set his magnificent craftsmen copying original prototypes from the mainland —even though these were technically inferior.[105]

For the reader who wishes to study the chronological problem further I have reproduced, on p. 34, Furumark's date-scheme for Mycenean pottery:[106] this has managed to survive a whole series of divergent hypotheses, and is still serviceable despite the time that has elapsed since it was first published, in 1941—the finest tribute anyone could wish for to its author's impartial objectivity. Its findings for the mainland complement the Cretan date-scheme I have already put forward. Again, we may note that it does not go back beyond 1550 (as opposed to 2200 for Crete), a fact which needs some explaining if one rejects the postulate of two successive mainland invasions.

This long period of peace and prosperity, lasting several hundred years and untroubled by external enemies, is sufficient explanation by itself for two phenomena: first the overpopulation from which the Achaean world suffered after 1400, and which led to the extraordinary

MYCENAEAN POTTERY

Mycenaean I	1550–1500
,, IIA	1500–1450
,, IIB	1450–1425
,, IIIA1	1425–1400
,, IIIA2 primitive	1400–1375
,, IIIA2 late	1375–1300
,, IIIB	1300–1230
,, IIIC1 primitive	1230–1200
,, IIIC1 late	1200–1125
,, IIIC2	1125–1100

rationing scheme revealed by the Linear B tablets; and, secondly, the unwarlike nature of these people, who in nearly eight hundred years of history made no conquests apart from Crete and Rhodes. (Even so, as we shall see, the conquest of Rhodes was forced upon the Achaeans, and more or less fortuitous.) The fact that the Achaeans never brought other peoples into subjection likewise explains the surprising fact that Bronze Age society—like Homeric society—contained very few slaves.

It is very curious to see that in the whole Achean world there is only one attested instance of voluntary colonisation: Sarpedon's departure from Crete, with his followers, to found Miletus. This remedy for overpopulation, which the Greeks employed systematically from the ninth century B.C. onwards, seems not to have struck anyone as being even worthy of consideration. The Achaeans built Cyclopean fortresses to defend themselves against each other; but none of them thought of striking out adventurously into the still more or less empty world that lay just beyond their horizon. Here we are confronted with a somewhat baffling problem. Why did the Achaeans never colonise Italy, which lies scarcely further from the Peloponnese than Crete? Why did they rather choose to dig themselves in behind those gigantic ramparts, till chronic overpopulation choked the life out of them for ever? Perhaps life in Greece was too attractive to them, so that no one was willing to sacrifice himself, and they all kept waiting for each other to take the plunge instead, like nineteenth-century European powers with their colonial empires. Perhaps: who will ever know?

At all events, the colossal fortifications that these people erected shortly after 1400—with scarcely any slave manual labour at their disposal, and using the most primitive techniques—prove that there was an abundant labour force available round the turn of the century: especially when we consider the speed with which the work was completed. The ring-wall of Gla, in Boeotia, is some 3500 yards in circumference, with a minimum thickness of five yards and an average height of six—not to mention the watch-towers and the two palaces which it contains. Hundreds of thousands of labourers must have been employed to shift those titanic stone blocks. It is hardly surprising that the generations after the Dark Ages could not believe they were looking at the work of mere mortals: after the Dark Ages the overpopulation that had begun about 1400 was quite forgotten. Yet in Attica alone, which was never a fertile area,[107] there were well over thirty Mycenaean settlements.[108]

These people, despite the discovery of weapons in some early Achaean graves, do not appear to have been a particularly warlike race. Let me again emphasise the total absence of fortifications until about 1350. They lived in open villages, and it seems probable that Grave Circles A and B contain the bodies of village chieftains, from settlements in the neighbourhood of Mycenae.[109] The fact that Greece has yielded up countless tombs of the Geometric Period, but very few from the Bronze Age, merely shows us that in the Bronze Age only chieftains received burial of a permanent nature: the vast majority were shovelled under the bare earth, and left no trace behind them—a phenomenon which can be observed, to a still more marked degree, in Troy. But in the Geometric Period each person was buried in a grave made from a few large stones, and containing some pieces of pottery, both of them substances resistant to decay. However, we cannot draw any conclusions as to the size of the population from this evidence.[110]

A large proportion of the arms found in these Achaean graves are ceremonial weapons, of nugatory value in actual combat. Two funerary *stelae* show us an Achaean, driving his chariot single-handed after a foot-soldier and endeavouring to run him through with his lance. To anyone with the slightest knowledge of Greek and, *a fortiori*, Cretan topography it will be obvious that such fighting tactics must have been inefficient to a degree. The lack of discipline among the small herdsmen, whom the central government never succeeded in controlling properly, is not difficult to account for when one thinks of the way that control was exercised. The very idea of chasing a goatherd through Arcadia by chariot, and single-handed, is inherently ludicrous. (Plate 2)

The united forces of all Achaea took ten years to capture Troy VIIa; yet archaeological evidence shows that this was nothing but a hastily patched-up fortress. Already by Thucydides' day Achaean methods of warfare were considered lamentably ineffectual.[111] In Homer the heroes square up to each other in single combat, while the troops stand and watch, judging each blow with an expert and appreciative eye. Chariots are reduced to the status of glorified cabs. This is a tournament between nobles, not a war. The reason why the Achaeans were so loud in singing the praises of the heroic outlook (which freed man from countless taboos and superstitions) is, in all likelihood, because they enjoyed celebrating virtues they did not themselves possess. This is a widespread and rather endearing fault; one could find endless examples of it in present-day society.

Fortunately, we possess written evidence from their own hand, which shows them to have been niggling, over-scrupulous bureaucrats. So there are two groups of documents from which we can form our opinion on their character: the tradition given permanent shape by Homer, some five centuries after they disappeared, and their own contemporary account-books. The epic version is undoubtedly more attractive, and has enchanted countless generations: many people have modelled their own conduct on it. But the historian cannot but pore over the figures in those accounts and draw his own conclusion from them. They are irrefutable. A falsehood may grow more venerable with time, but that does not make it any the truer. Contemporary documents always constitute a potential threat to tradition: when the Dead Sea scrolls are finally deciphered in their entirety, will it not be necessary to rewrite the whole history of Christianity?

It is interesting, in this context, to compare Homer's epic poems with the Byzantine epic *Digénis Akritas*, which attempted to fulfil an analogous role for a later age. This poem—or rather the rhapsodes who composed it—created, *ex nihilo*, the heroic Byzantine mentality which all our other sources (and they are plentiful for the tenth and eleventh centuries A.D.) contradict at every point. Digénis Akritas never existed, nor was he modelled on any living person; he simply embodied all the unrealisable dreams of his contemporaries. Unfortunately the Byzantine rhapsodes were bad poets, and their epic uniformly boring; but the ideal attitude to life which *Digénis Akritas* reveals is very curious indeed. The only recognised sins are those of a sexual nature; and, in order to purify himself after one such lapse, Digénis at one point actually kills the woman he has just violated. This absolves him from his guilt. The story abounds in fantastic architecture and fairy-tale gardens; and the feats performed by Achilles are the merest child's play when compared with those of Digénis, who invariably fights singlehanded and (of course) works his way through whole armies without ever becoming exhausted.[112] He belongs to a noble caste which had no factual existence; and when we set this folklore for illiterates beside the precise, rather dry prose of Constantine Porphyrogenitus, it is impossible not to regret that Agamemnon's memoirs have failed to survive, as a corrective to the Homeric *Iliad*: the comparison would have proved most enlightening. But all we in fact possess are his accounts.

These Achaean nobles were scarcely what one might call turbulent—certainly not by the standards of the Middle Ages, when every fortified castle was in arms against its neighbour. Only the Cadmean dynasty incurred the Greeks' implacable hatred, and with good cause.[113] They annihilated them in two campaigns; but on the whole this archaic world seems to have been spared the destructive horrors of civil war. The Achaeans were marvellous artists, and must have loved their splendid festivals: the races, the athletic contests, the divine poetry that was sung to them by their bards. Their dramas generally hinged on sexual relationships or religious problems. But the spirit of adventure and conquest seems never to have fired their hearts. They did, it is true, fight one major planned campaign, the famous Trojan War; but, as I hope to demonstrate, they only decided to do so under the pressure of most exigent necessity. What is more, they went about it so incompetently that one can hardly picture anyone doing worse; they several times came within an ace of defeat; and in the end they straggled back to their palaces, where they lived peacefully for another couple of generations. We hear very little more of them after this. If we possessed no evidence but the *Chansons de Geste*, what picture would we get of our own Middle Ages—which are, by comparison, much closer to us in time?

These heroes who never conquered anyone were hardly in a position to own slaves. Where would they have found them? Even when they subjugated Crete, we have not the slightest reason to suppose that they reduced one single Cretan to slavery. There were probably a few captives acquired as a result of raids or shipwrecks, but their numbers must have been insignificant. Besides, in a society where food was severely rationed, a slave was one extra mouth to feed. Here the evidence of the Homeric poems and the Linear B tablets is in agreement. Reference to slaves do indeed occur, but most of them concern 'slaves of the Gods', *te-o-jo do-e-ro* or *Theoîo doûloi*,[114] who are in a position to rent holdings; Ventris and Chadwick themselves think that these persons were not slaves in the full sense which the word later came to acquire, but free second-class citizens, perhaps those who farmed temple land.[115] I think myself we can go further, and identify these 'slaves' [*doûloi*][116] with the peasant class, who are not mentioned by any other title, though their holdings are painstakingly catalogued,[117] and all other crafts, such as smith, baker, weaver, and so on, are enumerated with the greatest care. We could almost identify this group by a simple process of elimination; but what virtually clinches the argument is the fact that a *doûlos* at Pylos received only half-rations (that is, a pint or half-litre of corn), and would very soon have starved to death if he had not been a peasant, and therefore, in all likelihood, someone with other sources of nutriment such as meat or milk.[118] We may note in passing that though cheese is referred to by the tablets, they make no mention of milk. This is probably due to the latter's perishable nature: it must have been consumed on the spot by the peasant-slaves and the shepherds.

We should also note that, in contradistinction to Troy, neither Crete nor mainland Greece have yielded up any bread-ovens—thus confirming Hesiod's remark about the first Greeks of the Bronze Age.[119]

So any individual slave-owner would have to be someone with the right to a holding of land, who was—provided the Palace authorities approved—using another person to cultivate it for him. It seems to me that if neither the Homeric world nor that revealed by the Linear B tablets contained slaves, we can with some confidence conclude that slavery as such was virtually non-existent in Achaean society.[120]

I would like to emphasise, at this juncture, the very considerable part played during the Bronze Age by another domestic creature, all too often neglected by historians: the bee. The tablets—already somewhat late evidence for the period I am concerned with here—make frequent mention of honey-offerings to various deities: offerings which seem somewhat excessive if their only purpose was to act as a food-sweetener.[121] But the bee, from time immemorial, was always associated with the bull—a fact one too often forgets.[122] The complex mythology which had finally woven itself round these two creatures persisted for hundreds of years thereafter. Virgil, in the first century B.C., still knew these legends; he even still believed that bees could be generated spontaneously in the carcase of a ritually slaughtered bull.[123] There is one aspect of this curious tradition which has a special interest for us here: Virgil claims that the man who discovered this miraculous way of obtaining bees was none other than Aristeus, the first King of Arcadia.

Now Aristeus was a historical figure, whose *floruit* can be placed shortly after 1400 B.C. He married Autonoë, one of the daughters of Cadmus, King of Thebes—a union which formed the basis for important political developments, as we shall see presently.[124] According to legend, Aristeus was the son whom the nymph Cyrene bore to Apollo. Now in Homer Apollo is the anti-Achaean god *par excellence*, who invariably fights in the Trojan ranks, along with Artemis and Aphrodite. This is no more than we might expect. As we shall see, Delphi had been a Theban possession up till the war of the Epigoni; and Apollo, despite the recent fall of the Cadmean dynasty, still belonged to the Dionysiac group of deities, together with his sister Artemis and—it goes without saying—voluptuous Aphrodite, whom the rhapsode does not fail to ridicule, lover and all.

But the nymph Cyrene was herself the daughter of Hypsaeus,[125] King of the Lapiths, a savage race which fought against the Centaurs,[126] the latter being glorified Achaean horses. All this fits in perfectly with the marriage of Aristeus, which gave him an *entrée* to the Cadmean royal family—a dynasty in mortal opposition to that of Mycenae. For the moment, however, let us merely note that the association between bees and bulls goes back at least to the middle period of the Bronze Age.

In this connection we should not forget that the *omphalos* at Delphi was a stone shaped like a beehive. Its surface was decorated with a raised *carrelage* which might represent either a net (such as we see on the Vapheio cups, its purpose being to capture wild bulls) or the cells of a honeycomb. Pausanias[127] tells us that the second[128] temple at Delphi was built of wax, by bees, and decorated with feathers—the latter perhaps an allusion to the sacred doves which figure so largely in Minoan art. The temple, then, was a beehive, and it was from this that the *omphalos* derived its shape.

It was beneath this sacred *omphalos*, which had the double function of a temple and a tomb, that Zagreus was buried after being torn to pieces by the Titans. From here he was resurrected as the god of flock-fertility, whose business it was to ensure reproduction in season.[129] This myth concerning the 'beehive' temple is beyond doubt the reason why, during the period under discussion, distinguished persons had themselves buried—as their god was buried—in beehive tombs. Could it be that they hoped to achieve a resurrection akin to that obtained by their fertility-spirit?

The sacred character which the first herdsmen attributed to the bee-hive stemmed from the fact that their particular intoxicating and prophetic liquor was hydromel, the Celtic mead—honey dissolved in water and then fermented. This was the reason why so much honey was distributed to the god's acolytes, as the Pylos and Cnossos tablets tell us. The mere fact that the second temple at Delphi was a sacred bee-hive is proof enough both that by the period under discussion the Achaeans were settled in Phocis, and that their Delphic prophecies were uttered under the influence of hydromel.[130] The reasons for my belief that wine was introduced into Greece about the mid-fourteenth century I shall discuss in their proper place; here I only wish to emphasise the importance (to us, perhaps, somewhat exaggerated) which intoxicating liquors, and the mysterious properties they possessed, had for men in those far-off times.

We should never forget that there existed then only one specific against every kind of physical or mental suffering: drunkenness. In one tomb (gamma) of Grave Circle B at Mycenae there was found the skull of a man who had been trepanned—and survived the operation. Many jaw-bones display the characteristic cellular pits left by dental abcesses, which cause excruciating pain; and there must have been a thousand other cruel sufferings which assailed these people but left no archaeologically discernible traces behind. Since alcohol was the one thing which enabled them to forget, if only for a little, the harsh realities of their day-to-day existence, it is very natural that they should have credited it with magical properties; and the fact that the beehive acquired a sacred character, as the source of this beneficent and intoxicating honey-drink, follows inevitably from the first premise. From here it is only one further step to associate this sacred, prophetic, and consolatory beehive with the god of flock-fertility, Zagreus, who safeguarded the livelihood of the tribe; and that step, as we have seen was undoubtedly taken in the Bronze Age, with the setting up of oracular Achaean sanctuaries at Delphi.

Even during the classical period we can still catch a faint echo of this belief in the sovereign powers of intoxication, particularly from Euripides' *Bacchae*.[131] By this time wine had, of course, replaced hydromel as the common alcoholic beverage,[132] and Dionysus, as we shall see, had been merged with Zagreus. But the fervour itself remained identical. In his play Euripides does not by any means present Dionysus in a favourable light. The god is selfish, cruel, and vindictive; yet men must worship him, with all his faults, and submit to his will, however absurd, even when he sets frail and venerable old men dancing, for it is he, the Lord Dionysus, who has brought mankind their one defence against pain of body or mind: 'A God himself, he is poured to the Gods as a libation, and so through him mankind receive all the good that befalls them.' There could not be a plainer identification of the god and the intoxicating liquor as such: wine, hydromel and *kykéon* all acquire characteristics of the divine. This tribute to the quality of unreason which the wine bestows, rendered at the end of the fifth century B.C. by the most rational of all Greek poets, may help us to appreciate what magical powers men who lived a thousand years earlier must have attributed both to the assuaging, prophetic condition of drunkenness *per se*, and to the means by which that condition was induced.

This was how cattle-farmers came to keep bees;[133] in due course we shall see how, and why, goatherds took up viticulture.

The contrast between rich and poor, and the way of life which each led, was accentuated still further by the different sacred liquors they employed. In Greece the vine does poorly in the plains, but flourishes on hillsides. However, if we are to discover the reasons for the mounting pressure which finally drove this cultivated, sedentary society to embark on its great venture against Troy, we must first turn our attention for a little to the north-west extremity of Asia Minor; unless we are acquainted with the conditions prevailing in this area towards the close of the Bronze Age, we cannot hope to understand why events in Greece developed as they did.

Unfortunately the history of Troy is, archaeologically speaking, one of the most complex processes known to man. The site was occupied continuously between 3200 and 1100 B.C., then abandoned, and only

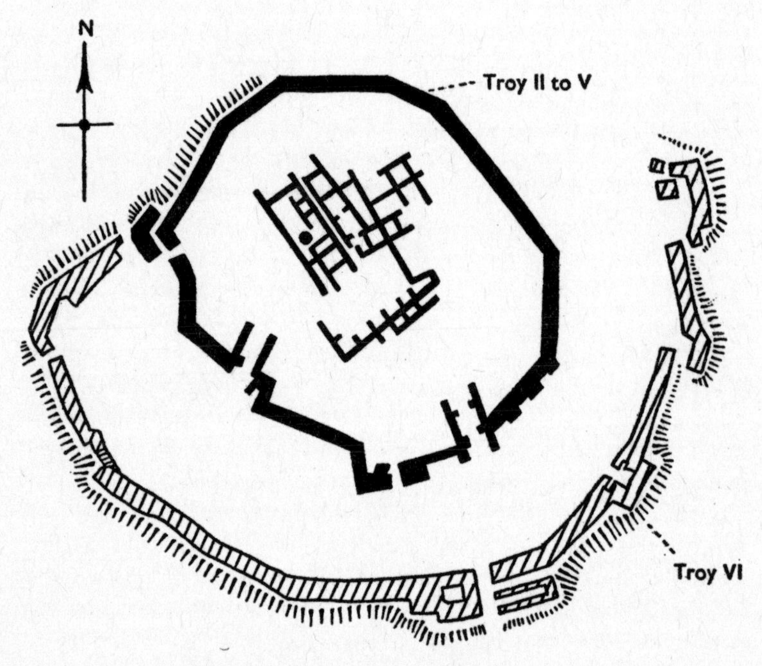

A sketch of the ground plan of Troy

reoccupied from about 720.[134] Scholars now commonly distinguish eight different stratigraphical levels, which can be dated, within approximate limits, as follows: Troy I, 3200–2600; Troy II, 2600–2300; Troy III, 2300–2200; Troy IV, 2200–2050; Troy V, 2050–1900; Troy VI, 1900–1300; Troy VIIa, 1300–1240; Troy VIIb, 1240–1100; Troy VIII, after 720.

During this long history Troy underwent many vicissitudes, which I shall not attempt to describe here. The famous treasure unearthed by Schliemann dated from Troy II. The Greeks destroyed Troy VIIa. From Troy I on, the imported pottery shows most grounds for comparison with Early Helladic II. Most of these phases overlapped with one or more periods of construction. The major break was between Troy V and Troy VI. Hitherto Troy had been no more than a fortress, large enough to shelter the sovereign and a few leading families. But the surface area of Troy VI is greatly extended (between three and four times the size of Troy V) and we find ourselves confronted with something very like the later Mycenean formula: a fortress complete with royal palace and a vast inner enclosure, where the neighbouring population, plus their cattle, could take refuge in time of trouble. But Troy VI is still very small by comparison with any similar Achaean establishment. The circumference of its walls was between 400 and 500 yards, as against 700 for Athens, 800 for Tiryns, 1100 for Mycenae, and 3500 for Gla. Troy VI must have been a city of quite exceptional magnificence; yet no trace of precious metal, either gold or silver, has come to light in it.

The men who built Troy VI made Minyan pottery, which turns up abundantly at this level. These newcomers also introduced the horse, and, it would appear, remained on amicable terms with the inhabitants of Troy V, since there is no trace of destruction or burning. Troy VI poses much the same problems as confront us in mainland Greece. Did the occupants arrive in one wave or two? And were the first immigrants, those who fashioned Minyan ware, Greek or Luwian? (It is more or less certain that the second group was Greek.) But the greatest mystery surrounding Troy is the fact that the Trojans do not appear to have buried their dead. Only one small cemetery of cinerary urns has been found there, some 500 yards from the citadel: this would seem to have belonged to Troy V. Yet the length of time during which the site was occupied, and the splendour of Troy VI, which survived for 600 years, both suggest, beyond reasonable doubt, that more than a million people must have died in or near the city. What, then, has become of their remains? No one knows. In any case the absence of tombs makes reconstructing Trojan history a particularly difficult and hazardous task. Furthermore, the Trojans either were illiterate, or else wrote on perishable materials such as wood or leather, since no inscriptions survive. The architecture of Troy VI is far more elegant than Mycenaean architecture, and less megalithic: the impression it conveys is, almost, one of luxury. The Achaeans built in a utilitarian fashion, solely to defend themselves. The rulers of Troy cared somewhat more for appearances.

Troy kept itself in isolation from the Asiatic world (with which, in any case, it lacked good natural communications); in particular, the Trojans seem to have had no acquaintance with the Hittite monarchs, who were equally ignorant concerning them—though they knew all about Tlepolemus's Achaean kingdom on Rhodes.[135] Apart from two small cylinder-seals, not one of the numerous artifacts discovered in the Troy VI stratum could possibly have an Oriental origin. All the imports are Mycenean, the bulk of them (fragments of over 700 vases have been found, despite the small area dug) luxury articles such as drinking cups. This demonstrates the close cultural affinities existing between Troy and the Aegean world.

Horses apart, the Trojans also—as Blegen has pointed out[136]—bred small livestock on a very considerable scale. The abundance of bones, of both sheep and goats, that have been found at every level in Troy VI shows that there was certainly no shortage of wool. Furthermore, Schliemann dug up no less than 7737 spindle-weights in Troy, and Blegen another 400, thus proving that the basic industry of Ilium was weaving, and that what kept the city commercially prosperous was, primarily, its fabrics, which seem to have been unrivalled throughout the eastern Mediterranean.

As I have said, we are particularly ill-informed over all matters pertaining to the Trojans. We possess neither their tombs nor their writing; the only place where they come to life for us is in the *Iliad*. It is hard to make the proper allowance here for poetic distortion in the absence of any corrective document; but the Homeric epics do presuppose a great similarity between Trojans and Achaeans. Priam possesses a harem, and what appears to have been a mercenary army:[137] when the troops raise a great shout, there are so many men from different lands, speaking such a variety of languages, that one could not but be astounded at their clamour.[138] This shows, moreover, that the actual citizens of Troy could not have been very numerous—a con-

3 The walls of Troy VI

4 The remains of Troy VIIa (two views). Note in the upper photograph the sunken cists (one with a lid in situ)

clusion supported by the dimensions of their fortress. However, the epithet 'barbarian', i.e. non-Greek, seems to be used by Homer as an insult rather than for purposes of racial distinction; and besides, the Trojans had more or less the same gods as the Greeks, with regular aid and support, as we have already seen, from the Dionysiac group. They were, primarily, small livestock breeders, but perhaps also possessed bulls on a large enough scale for Zeus to hesitate before condemning them out of hand.

The Trojans offer the same sacrifices as the Achaeans, with an identical form of ritual. Most of their names are also to be found in the Pylos tablets as the names of Pylians, and this can scarcely be accidental. Better still, Erichthonius and Dardanus are given a royal pedigree in both contexts. Obviously it will not do to press the theory too far as regards detail; but whatever its previous history, and despite its stubbornly persistent tendency to go on turning out Minyan ware, we can say that after six hundred years of continuous existence Troy VI was a kingdom inhabited by men who were strongly Hellenised if not actually Greek; whose staple occupation was the breeding of horses and small livestock; and who made the latter the basis for a flourishing weaving industry, through which they were enabled to import luxury articles, though only from the Mycenean world.

The splendour that was Troy VI vanished for ever in a terrible earthquake about the year 1300 B.C. Troy VIIa represents a direct continuation of Troy VI, but of the old magnificence not a trace remains. The walls were patched up in a makeshift fashion, and all the available space inside was crammed with small dwellings, often built with material taken from the previous town. Another characteristic of Troy VIIa is that almost every house, however modest, contains anything between one and twenty jars [*pithoi*], so deeply buried in the ground that not more than three or four inches were visible, and each equipped with a flat stone by way of a lid. Here we have tangible evidence of preparations to withstand the possibility of a siege. Streets become narrow and winding; buildings encroach on the public squares. The palace must have been a miserable affair: it is no longer recognisable. Grey Minyan ware continued to be produced, but this impoverished society could no longer import the splendid Mycenean pottery which had been the show-pieces of every banquet when Troy VI still stood. Such luxury ware as exists is a poor-quality imitation, manufactured locally.[139] The weaving industry must have collapsed, and there was no longer any surplus capital available for imports. This point, which

I shall touch on again later, is of vital importance for understanding the factors that drove the Achaeans to undertake the Trojan War. Troy VIIa disappeared in a vast conflagration brought about by the hand of man; its inhabitants must have been exterminated, since Troy VIIb (after a few timid attempts to follow in the tradition of VIIa) reveals, in its uppermost stratum, the arrival of altogether new occupants, who brought bucchero ware with them. The Achaeans had achieved their desired end.

Such, in brief outline, is the historical structure of Troy's second main period as a city. Having described it I need not refer to it again, and can now embark, without further interruption, on the history of the Achaean world towards the end of the Bronze Age. As we have seen, prolonged peace had brought about a steady expansion of trade between Greece and Crete—the size of which we can guess at when we examine the treasures that chieftains from unfortified Achaean villages had buried with them. This expansion continued until about 1450; but from then on the importation of Cretan artifacts by the mainland began to fall away, and ceased altogether shortly before 1400. The wealth of the Mycenaean world appears to have suddenly dried up. Here we have one of the surest indications of that dangerous population increase which was beginning to threaten the Achaean world. Peace had lasted a long time; the women were, clearly, all too fertile, and devoted to the worship of the Great Mother,[140] the goddess of fecundity; the men, insofar as we can tell from their skeletons, were handsome, virile specimens,[141] and the fine Greek climate did the rest.

But population explosions—as the contemporary world is only too well aware—pose a number of complicated problems, and the piecemeal methods by which the Achaeans attempted to solve their difficulty proved, in the end, a failure. The surplus population, driven up into the hills by the proprietors of the cramped if fertile plainland, began to give cause for alarm. After about a century they forced the rich stock-farmers to build their celebrated fortifications. There is no evidence for any external attack during this period; but the marked decline in what the wealthy could afford to buy shows how relentlessly they, together with their horses and their cattle, were harried by the starving herdsmen from the mountains. Such cattle, of course, would make an easy target, and could be destroyed in quantities during a nocturnal raid; whereas small lifestock such as sheep or goats can almost literally vanish into thin air.[142] The tension must have mounted further and further during this half-century of decline, till it culminated, about 1405, in the Cretan conquest of the Achaeans—a conquest brought about through one most vitally significant historical event, to which few scholars attach the importance it deserves.

To say in a metaphorical aside that the period between 1450 and 1400 was 'the calm before the storm' constitutes a totally meaningless platitude. Political storms, much less international ones, are never preceded by a calm: they are the product of mounting tensions which finally break out into violent conflict. In Greece, we find bull and goat more and more in opposition as time goes on, with Dionysus flouting the authority of Zagreus.[143]

The Dionysiac goat cult has left no archaeological traces that I know of. It has survived only in written evidence and in myths. But this is no more than we might expect. These wandering goat-people had nowhere to place permanent religious symbols. Ceremonial burials were certainly impossible for them; and as semi-nomads they can never have built real houses.

In contrast to the miserable life forced on the majority of the Greek continental population, it is during this period (that is between 1450 and 1400) that Cnossos produced what was perhaps its finest pottery, known as the 'Palace Style' because the superb examples of it which survive are almost wholly confined to the Palace of Minos. The model for this ceramic style, with its symmetrical decorative design, seems to have come from mainland Greece, where the great primitive beehive tombs contain similar pots, of local manufacture, which apparently predate the Cretan ware: the latter, in this case, would be no more than highly developed and refined copies.[144] Various hypotheses have been produced to explain this phenomenon, and these we must now examine, since they will affect the interpretation we arrive at for the events of 1405, which brought the Greeks, for the first time, on to the stage of history as we know it.

For many years it was fashionable to say that the Achaeans gradually conquered the whole of Crete, and that the last stronghold of resistance was Cnossos, which remained in isolation from 1450 to 1405, and went down still turning out immortal works of art. I see no useful purpose in pursuing this theory any further, since it no longer has more than a few rare adherents.

The modern view[145] is that about 1450 a first Achaean dynasty established itself in Cnossos, to be ousted by a local rebellion in 1405. This hypothesis is improbable *per se* and cannot, for a number of reasons, be maintained. To begin with, the killing of the Minotaur—and consequently Theseus's *floruit*—would have to be placed in about 1450. This is quite impossible. Archaeological evidence precludes our dating the synoecism universally associated with the name of Theseus before the beginning of the fourteenth century; and Theseus cannot, therefore, have killed the Minotaur in 1450. Furthermore, we should have to refute the detailed arguments which tend to produce a later date for the Linear B tablets;[146] and, as I have said before, to proclaim one's distaste for these arguments does not constitute a refutation of them.[147]

This theory of an early Greek dynasty in Cnossos, between 1450 and 1405, involves us in insuperable difficulties over the transmission of Linear B from Crete—where the script was first evolved from Linear A—to mainland Greece, where, according to this hypothesis, we find it between two hundred and two hundred and fifty years later, quite unchanged, at Pylos and Mycenae. If we accept the idea of an early Greek dynasty which reigned in Cnossos from 1450 to 1405, and employed the Linear B script, we have to concede the fact[148] that, after this local rebellion in 1405, during which the whole place was burnt and never rebuilt (why?), there was, for a long period, no Greek-speaking population in Crete. Here we have this mere handful of Achaeans, who developed Linear B from Linear A; how, after being destroyed utterly in 1405, were they able, two centuries later, to transmit the secret of an identical script to Mycenae and Pylos? This is a mystery no one has attempted to resolve, and with good reason. Finally we may ask ourselves how, with Cnossos then the most prosperous power in the Mediterranean world, this Achaean dynasty managed to seize power at all: it was not by force, for which archaeological evidence is wholly lacking. Some scholars have suggested persuasion; a somewhat unconvincing argument.[149]

Here Palmer's chronology seems to me irrefutable. Evans was wrong: the Achaeans destroyed Cnossos once only, in 1405, and rebuilt it *à la grecque*, that is, adapting the Throne Room for their own purposes. This—we have no reason to doubt Homer's word[150]—was the palace of Idomeneus.

The period we call Late Minoan III (1405–1100) corresponded with the flourishing rule of these Achaean kings, who were finally overthrown in 1100 by a Dorian-based revolution, as a result of which the palace was burnt for a second time. During this conflagration the Linear B tablets we possess were baked hard. These backward invaders never rebuilt the palace—a perfectly understandable fact in 1100, but quite inexplicable in 1405, when every circumstance favoured Cnossos.

Granted such conditions, there is only one possible *raison d'être* for the 'Palace Style'. It appears during a period of great material affluence and flourishing cultural activity, and must have been due to some Minoan sovereign with a passion for Greek art.[151] This art failed to catch on in the other Cretan palaces, and Cnossos took no steps to impose it on them. Perhaps, indeed, she was in no position to do so. We do not know how the Minoan world was organised; we cannot read Linear A; and the other palaces may have enjoyed far greater independence then than would appear from the world revealed by the Linear B tablets towards the close of the twelfth century, when chronic overpopulation had led (as they show us) to severe rationing.[152]

Here, more or less, is how we must picture the Graeco-Cretan world towards the end of the fifteenth century B.C. Crete was at the zenith of a long, increasingly powerful ascendancy. She possessed numerous commercial warehouses and a flourishing network of trade. As the magnificent 'Palace Style' shows us, she had never been so prosperous. She had completely recovered from the effects of the great earthquake in 1560, and her relations with Egypt remained unbroken. Her palaces were of unparalleled splendour, and her towns, with the Cretan fleet to protect them, needed no defensive walls.

On the mainland a quite different situation prevailed. The Achaeans were still living in unfired mud-brick villages, without fortifications, which clustered round the swampy plainland. Such areas were owned by the chieftains, who were buried in those ceremonial tombs we have already discussed, and whose main occupation was the breeding of cattle and horses. However, the large bulk of this ever-increasing population had been forced up into the hills, where they lived off their flocks of sheep and goats, leading the semi-nomadic existence which such a way of life invariably imposes on those who follow it. By the end of the century the opposition between the two classes must have become intense, and it seems likely that the general peace and prosperity had been disturbed since about 1450, since the country's purchasing power had dropped sharply, and imports had more or less stopped altogether. Architectural building, in so far as we can judge, was restricted to funerary and, perhaps, general religious requirements.[153]

It was now that an event occurred which was to have severe repercussions on the subsequent history of the Bronze Age peoples. Sicania, as the group of Minoan settlements in Sicily was known, flared up in revolt—why, we do not know—under the leadership of Daedalus, the craftsman-architect. This famous man probably helped the Sicilian cities to fortify themselves—a great novelty at this period—since the Cretan fleet which laid siege to Camicus failed in its attempt to reduce it. The Cretans were starving; they must have consumed all the flocks they brought with them as food-supplies. Worst of all, the King of Cnossos was killed, by Cocalus, King of Camicus. In the end the Cretans raised the siege, and tried to sail back to their own island; but a storm cast them up on the coast of Iapygia, in the heel of Italy, where they founded the town of Hyria. This name means 'of or belonging to the hive'[154] a most apposite choice for a settlement built by followers of the bull, and therefore also of the bee.[155] Theron, tyrant of Acragas at the beginning of the fifth century, was familiar with the story of Minos's death before his town of Camicus,[156] and Diodorus's description of the Cretan monarch's burial-place proves that the story must be genuine, for the tomb he describes is practically identical with the temple-tomb of Cnossos, which Diodorus could not possibly have known.[157] Furthermore, at Sant' Angelo Musaro, close to Acragas (the modern Agrigento), there are the remains of a Minoan necropolis.[158] It would seem, then, an indubitable fact that, shortly before 1400, a King of Crete brought an armada to Sicily, and besieged the island. The expedition was a failure, the king died in action, and the fleet was lost.

The loss of this squadron, together with its complement of men, must have seriously weakened—if not actually destroyed—the Cretan thalassocracy under whose protection that magnificent phase of Minoan culture had scope to flourish and develop. We see, too, that the last Egyptian reference to Keftiu (Crete) is about 1405, since the inscription was carved on the occasion of Tuthmosis IV's funeral.[159] The Tell-el-Amarna texts make no further reference to Keftiu. The tide of history now turns abruptly against the Minoans, just before raising the Mycenaean empire to its highest pinnacle of success.[160]

The collapse of this maritime empire was far too good an opportunity for the bands of malcontents on the mainland to ignore, especially in view of the overpopulation prevailing there. It seems likely that they concerted their attacking forces, perhaps under the leadership of Theseus the Athenian, and that they carried all Crete before them: first Cnossos, Phaestus, Aghia Triadha and central Crete, then—as we have seen[161]—the whole of the island came under their sway. The details of this conquest, which subsequent historical events show to have been fairly rapid (perhaps taking no more than ten or twenty years), are hard to establish, and the present date-schemes somewhat contradictory.

At all events we may presume that among these hordes of Achaean adventurers who overran Crete there were both rich and poor, both followers of the bull and followers of the goat; plainsmen who feared that, what with overpopulation and raids by the mountain goatherds, they too would be ruined and forced to take to the hills, together with those who were already scraping a bare sustenance from the barren uplands themselves.

The followers of the goat, naturally enough, wanted nothing better than to set fire to all these unfortified palaces, with their flaunting taurine emblems. When we have witnessed the spectacle of a few individuals, during some riot or other, contriving to set whole districts of a modern city ablaze, it is not so much the destruction wrought by these men in Crete around the year 1405 that should surprise us, as the quantity of buildings and artifacts that in fact escaped disaster.

The followers of the bull, it goes without saying, took a wholly different attitude. They felt not the slightest hostility to the Minoans, whose culture—and perhaps whose language as well[162]—must have been so much akin to their own. The concepts of 'country' and 'fatherland' did not as yet exist, much less any notion of 'race'—as is graphically demonstrated by the history of those dynasties I shall deal with in my next chapter. Such affinities as there were must have existed more in their religious observances and their general mode of life. We know very little about Mycenaean religion. Zeus was the Father, the god of storms, the Thunderer; yet at the same time he had the title 'Dictaeus', which recalled his birth in a cave on Mount Dicté in Crete.[163] Zeus was a bull-god, besides being the father of Zagreus, and his followers had not the slightest intention of allowing themselves to be robbed of the fruits of their victory. Crete was a rich, flourishing land, and its exploitation would be a magnificent prize, probably the finest obtainable at the time. The followers of the goat were eliminated, and those of the bull quickly made good the damage done during the conquest—though they did so far adapt the palace to their own purposes as to introduce the idea of the Greek *megaron*, which now appears for the first time in Cretan architecture. Then they settled down to enjoy their newly won acquisitions.

From all we know it would appear that these bull-worshipping Achaeans were on excellent terms with their new subjects. There is nothing which suggests that they introduced either a social caste system or slavery. They were first-class administrators, with a shrewed eye to their own interests, as the Linear B tablets reveal; and during the century and a half of peace which elapsed between the fall of Cnossos and the Trojan War, Crete experienced the same sort of population explosion as had previously turned the Achaeans themselves into adventurers, and driven them to launch their assault on the great Aegean island. The demographic trend must have closely paralleled that of the mainland, since Crete's geography is much like that of the Peloponnese. Such rich plains as exist in Crete are of limited extent, and cannot support a dense population. The surplus was bound to be driven out into the hills—which here culminate in high mountain ranges, as majestic as they are wild and barren. From the moment the Greeks seized power, the spirit of adventure which had animated the Minoans promptly evaporated. There was no further colonising; the goods in the warehouses dwindled away, and Egypt was forgotten. Very soon the tendency towards a policy of inturned isolation becomes apparent. Yet these Achaean chieftains, for all that they had monopolised the palaces, and the rich plainland, and the island's cattle-farming, must nevertheless have found themselves, as time went on, under the same increasing pressure from the mountain-dwellers (who were virtually beyond authority's reach) as their fellow chieftains on the mainland. Otherwise they would never have allowed themselves to be dragged into those preventive wars of the Bronze Age which we shall examine presently.

Since the middle of Late Minoan II, and throughout the whole of Late Minoan III, Cretan architects had found themselves obliged to design door-frames in plaster-work rather than cypress wood, as previously, this change being brought about by the destruction of the forests with which Crete had once been covered. The destruction itself must, in all likelihood, be connected with the increasing proliferation of the goat. These animals made reafforestation schemes practically impossible, and the cypresses which grew so thick on Minos's island took a long time to reach maturity. Unbroken peace and good Achaean administration, coupled with a lack of the adventurous spirit, once more produced that most tricky hazard—overpopulation. Just as on the mainland, this phenomenon very soon divided the inhabitants into rich and poor, according to the type of district where they had settled.

But there was one fundamental difference between the two cases.

The Achaean chieftains on the mainland managed to muster a large enough labour force for the erection of immense, Cyclopean walls in order to defend themselves against their enemies' raids. Nothing of the sort exists in Crete. Yet the expedition of Sarpedon, the rigorous rationing system introduced by the palace administration, the Cnossos tablets concerning non-payment of taxes by sheep-owners, and the final disaster of 1100, all suggest that the problem of overpopulation must have been acute. In these circumstances the absence of all genuine fortifications is even more astonishing.

My own belief is that we must attribute this phenomenon to the comparatively small number of Achaeans who, it would appear, settled in Crete. They must, beyond a doubt, have established themselves as the superior ruling class of the island: otherwise it would be hard to understand how they managed to impose their architectural preferences and highly idiosyncratic methods of administration. But their subjects were for the most part Minoans—a race not given to the construction of megalithic fortresses—who would, surely, have rebelled if such a labour had been forcibly imposed on them. Slaves were rare and precious, and citizens of Achaean stock probably too few to undertake such a gigantic task.[164]

CHAPTER III

The Dawn of History

As I have attempted to demonstrate, animals played no less an important part than men in the Bronze Age; and, as we shall see, their deification in fertility rites prolonged their influence far beyond the period examined here. Of course, the further we move forward down the centuries, the greater the importance attached to agriculture; but throughout the period with which we are here concerned the products of the soil must have remained in comparative short supply, which is the only possible explanation for their severe rationing. The dramatic effect of the social cleavage imposed by two conflicting types of stock-farming first becomes apparent in the early years of the fourteenth century: this is how it came about.

As we saw above, once the Achaeans had secured Crete and reconstructed it after their own fashion, their next task must have been to replace the fleet that the last Minoan king of Crete had lost—though they were never to re-establish the Cretan maritime empire, or even to attempt to do so. Then they turned their eyes further afield. Some forty years after the conquest of Crete, about 1360—according to the synoptic date-scheme I have evolved, which I shall follow and explain henceforward—King Taurus (whom legend identified with Zeus) taking advantage of the absence on an expedition of the local monarch, Agenor, seized Tyre and carried off Europa as his captive.[165] According to tradition Europa was, as we have seen, the daughter of Phoenix,[166] the eponymous founder of the Phoenicians. Taurus built the great city of Gortyn in Crete for Europa—this was the only fortified city in the whole island[167]——and here she gave birth to the first Greek Minos. On his return Agenor, determined to avenge the wrong inflicted on the people of Tyre, dispatched a powerful squadron commanded by his son Cadmus, with the task of bringing back the fugitive. But this Tyrian force never disembarked in Crete.[168] Cadmus first made for Thera,[169] which—so far—suggests a normal enough route, bearing in mind the type of vessel employed at this period.

5a Amphoras found in a Canaanite cellar photographed in situ

b The tomb of a Mycenæan lady found in the Acropolis of Athens (reconstruction)

6a The crushed death-mask of a cyclops

b The death-mask of a cyclops

But before following the expedition of Cadmus any further, we should note that both he and his sailors undoubtedly belonged to the goat-worshipping faction. Tradition has enshrined this fact in the universally attested myth that Dionysus was born of the union between one of Cadmus's daughters, Semele, and Zeus.[170] Dionysus was originally the god of fecundity, of the generative principle in beasts and crops;[171] and as such he was particularly associated with the vine, from which the Tyrians obtained their magical and intoxicating liquor. The vine was cultivated in the northern part of their country, above all in the province of Canaan: this was not far from the port of Ugarit, where there was an important Minoan colony, and, it would seem, an Achaean settlement, the latter established at about the period with which we are here concerned. This cultivation of the vine must go back at least a hundred years before Cadmus's expedition,[172] since an Egyptian tomb-painting of the mid-fifteenth century[173] shows us raiders from Egypt carrying off numerous jars containing wine mixed with honey. Greece itself does not appear to have known wine before the fourteenth century, and it is likely that it was Cadmus and his followers who introduced viticulture there. At Athens there has been discovered the tomb of an Achaean noblewoman[174] which contained, *inter alia*, an amphora of Canaan wine, together with a 'Palace Style' jar of local manufacture. The fact that this distinguished lady imported her wine from Ugarit—which at the time must have been no small undertaking—suggests that by 1400 or thereabouts Greece was still not itself a wine-producing country. In any case wine must have been a rare luxury for this amphora to be deemed worthy of inclusion amongst an aristocrat's treasures.

Let us now return to the adventures of Cadmus and his Tyrians: wine-drinkers, goat-followers, worshippers of Dionysus. We left them at Thera, the modern Santorini. We have to assume that the Cretan fleet had, by 1360, become a force to be reckoned with once more, since the punitive expedition came no closer to its destination than this point. Our Tyrians subsequently turn up in Thebes,[175] where Cadmus was to found a powerful dynasty that afterwards played a vitally important part in late Bronze Age history.

How did Cadmus get from Thera to Thebes? It is unlikely that his small squadron was able to disembark direct at some Boeotian port,[176] and it seems out of the question that these followers of the goat could have recruited support amongst the Boeotians themselves, since their province was a flourishing centre, probably *the* centre,[177] of bull-worship. But support Cadmus needed, if he was to make himself master of Thebes, the city founded at the turn of the century by Amphion and Zethus (the sons of Zeus by the nymph Antiope[178]), and which must, even by then, have attained a certain importance. We need do no more than examine the remarkable ruins of Orchomenus and the vast Cyclopean ring-wall at Gla—inside which stand two palaces and a gigantic colonnade[179]—to realise how densely populated the area round Lake Copaïs must have been. If the Tyrians had approached the lake from the eastern side, it is hard to believe that they would have got past it without let or hindrance.

Tradition has it that before Cadmus[180] reached Thebes, he first secured possession of Delphi. In this case he would have crossed the mountains of Phocis—almost certainly a friendly country, where the tribes must have depended on sheep and goats for their livelihood, and from whose inhabitants Cadmus might well have drawn the reinforcements that enabled him to conquer Thebes. The city lay close to the pass, immediately below the uplands on the south-east side of Lake Copaïs: no need, now, to take a long, circuitous route through hostile and thickly populated countryside. It looks very much as though the tradition that Cadmus's conquest of Thebes was launched from Delphi has some historical truth behind it.

But how did Cadmus get from Thera to Delphi in the first place? Once again, it looks as though we can rule out a coastal voyage round the hostile Peloponnese—especially since this was a period when inshore navigation meant frequent halts, and hauling one's ships ashore almost every night. A reasonable solution to the problem can, perhaps, be reached by bringing two traditions together: that which asserts the prior conquest of Delphi, and that[181] which tells us how one of Cadmus's daughters, Autonoë, married Aristaeus, the future king of Arcadia. Arcadia, by the very nature of its terrain, was undoubtedly an important region for raising sheep and goats, and its inhabitants must, therefore, have been favourably disposed towards these adventurers from Tyre. One source,[182] a late one it is true, suggests that Aristaeus was responsible for the introduction of viticulture into Greece, and this would agree very well with his having married a member of the Cadmean dynasty.

It seems, therefore, not beyond the bounds of probability that the sequence of events was something like this. Faced with a far superior Cretan fleet, Cadmus gave up his expedition against Crete as impossible. But he could hardly, it was clear, return to Tyre empty-handed, and report the failure of his mission. He therefore disembarked, in quest of adventure, in the southern Peloponnese, probably at the foot of the east flank of Mount Taygetus; from here it is not too difficult a journey through the hill-country to Arcadia, and this route would avoid the cattle-breeding areas—hostile on principle to followers of the goat—whereas when he reached Arcadia, Agenor's son must have known he would find himself among friends.

Cadmus is presented to us by all our sources as an exceptional man,[183] and his story, as we shall see, does nothing to discredit this verdict. He was a great statesman and, above all, a first-class administrator, who was well aware of the most pressing problem his age had to deal with—namely, the appearance of a very large class of poor, discontented sheep and goat graziers. It is a reasonable assumption that he was responsible for organising his son-in-law Aristaeus's kingdom, in or about the year 1360; and that then, being determined to bring off a major *coup*, he seized Delphi, the main religious centre of the Achaeans. The occasion was marked by a log falling from heaven. Cadmus had this object encased in bronze and made people worship it as 'Cadmus Dionysus'.[184] He must have recruited followers without difficulty among the goat-breeders of Phocis; this combined force thereupon marched down from the mountains against Thebes, and captured it. The rich cattle-graziers settled in the plains must have felt most alarmed at the developments brought about by these damnable interlopers from Tyre. Since 1450, as we have already seen, increasing overpopulation had gradually divided the Achaean camp into two hostile groups. The opposition between them had tended to disorganise the administration, and this in turn jeopardised foreign trade. The situation took a sudden and dramatic turn for the 'rich' when the 'poor' began to organise themselves under the influence of these Cadmeans, who, *inter alia*, brought the art of viticulture with them.[185] (It must have been during this period that wine, once and for all, replaced hydromel at Delphi.)

To the cattle-graziers the danger must have seemed both imminent and extremely grave. It was more than lucky for them that at this juncture no external enemy—some still uncivilised tribe, perhaps, such as the Dorians—decided to march in and take advantage of the country's divided state. If Greece had not, at this epoch, been virtually isolated, we should have had no Mycenaean civilisation, no Homer, and in all likelihood no 'Greek miracle'. If things had fallen a little differently, Greece might well have become a Hittite province, for example. The Achaeans had a lucky escape on this score; but instead of going to the root of their trouble, and fighting overpopulation by the establishment of colonies for the surplus poor, these cattle-graziers set themselves so formidable a task that posterity for long attributed its execution to Titans, not believing that mere humans could have carried it through. In an unbelievably short space of time—not more than twenty or thirty years—the open villages in which the Greeks had lived for centuries became satellites grouped round a series of megalithic fortresses, which mostly appeared between 1360 and 1340.

Tiryns is especially interesting in this connection, since we can still trace the remains of three or four superimposed mud-brick villages there—on the fortified hill itself no less than around it. About 1350 the southern half of the hill was fortified, almost certainly by Perseus, at the same time as he was erecting the first ring-wall of Mycenae. This date also marks the building of the first palace, which was burnt a little after 1300—an event surely related to the change of Mycenaean dynasty in 1285, when the Danaïds were replaced by the Pelopidae. Not long afterwards the northern part of the hill was included in new fortifications: these were beyond doubt the work of Atreus, who in 1275 also built the second ring-wall of Mycenae. At Tiryns a vast enclosure was provided to serve as a refuge for the dwellers round about, together with their cattle.[186] The second palace—which so closely resembles

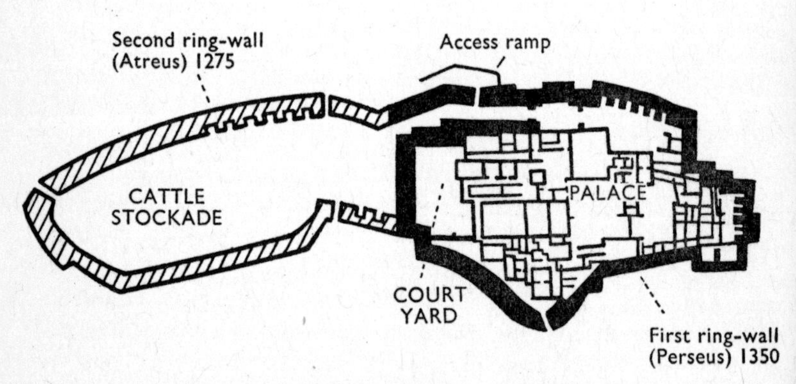

Sketch of the ground plan of Tiryns

Plate 7. A general view of Tiryns (*opposite this page*)

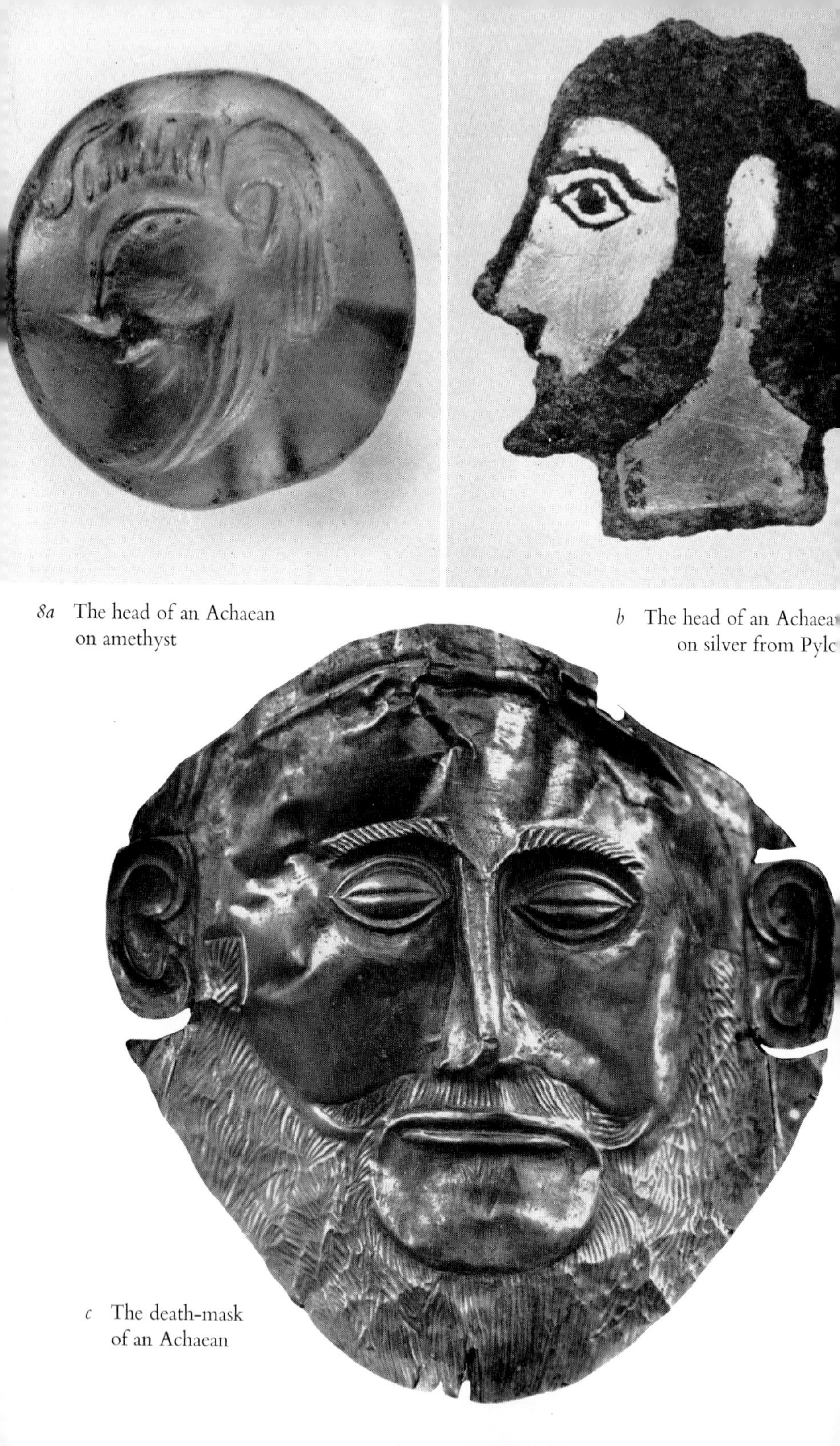

8a The head of an Achaean on amethyst

b The head of an Achaea on silver from Pylc

c The death-mask of an Achaean

Odysseus's palace as described by Homer—also dates from this period. The final destruction, like that of Mycenae, came in about 1160.[187].

The necropolis of Tiryns, situated less than a mile from the fortess itself, on the hill of St Elias, is exactly what one might expect: it contains shaft graves, tombs carved from the rock, and a domed vault which must have been reserved for the burial of Tiryns's sovereigns. As always in the Greek Bronze Age, the common people have left no trace of their passing.

The most curious remains at Tiryns are the pre-palatial foundations near the summit of the hill.[188] They seem to have belonged to a circular monument about eighty feet in diameter, which was roofed over with tiles and slates. This edifice must date back to before 1600, and is, so far as I know, unique of its kind. Was it employed for religious purposes?

At Orchomenus, too, it is possible to trace the remains of Middle as well as Late Helladic occupation in the area of the citadel: these unfortified villages were replaced, about 1400 or a little later, by a megalithic fortress contemporary with the ones at Mycenae and Tiryns. Iolcos [Iaōlkós], well away to the north, perhaps marks the furthest limit of the Achaean empire in this direction. Though excavation on the site has only recently begun, its majestic size is already apparent. Unfortunately the remains of the megalithic city lie directly beneath the modern town of Volos, which will make their exploration extremely difficult. The same, alas, applies to Thebes, where, nevertheless, three or four of the famous seven gates have been located, and the partial excavation of the Cadmeia has produced twenty-eight stirrup-jars bearing Linear B inscriptions.[189] As already mentioned,[190] the limited excavations now under way have yielded startling results.

Mention must also be made of the excavations at present being conducted on Ceos, since here, for the first time, something very like a temple has been discovered.[191] Gla and Athens belong to a slightly later period (*c.* 1275) and I shall deal with them in due course.

This incredible effort on the part of the Achaean plain-dwellers, and the speed with which it was accomplished, demonstrates the density of the population and the abundant labour-force that was, in consequence, available for the task. It is all the more striking when we recall that the existence of slaves on any considerable scale during the Greek Bronze Age is, to say the least, extremely problematical. But there is another puzzle here. The labour-force presupposed by these monumental constructions can be accounted for easily enough: it was brought into existence by the population explosion which two and a half centuries of comparative peace had created in the Achaean world. But how are we to explain the existence of a generation of expert architects, who appeared just at the moment when they were needed—men capable, moreover, of constructing the vaults of Tiryns, the Mycenaean ramparts, or the towers of Iolcos, and this with only the most primitive equipment at their disposal? The problem is one of some delicacy.

It has lately been suggested[192] that the architects who were capable of erecting these Cyclopean ramparts came from Lycia, where the walls of Boghazkeüy, the ancient Hittite capital Hattusa, display marked similarities—both in scale and the arrangement of gateways—with the fortresses erected by the Mycenaeans. They also antedate them somewhat, having been completed before 1350.[193] These Cyclopes [*Kyklōpes*] were, as their name indicates, people with large round eyes. Appellations deriving from peculiarities in the shape of the eye are very frequent among Greek names for races or peoples: we find Almopians, Cecropians, Mopsopians, Dryopians, Pelopians, and others.[194] (Plate 6.)

This hypothesis is certainly attractive; but the one tangible piece of evidence we possess is the tendency of the landless poor to gather round Cadmus's strong, magnetic personality, and join his Tyrian followers—a process which, about the mid-fourteenth century, obliged those whose wealth was tied up in cattle and real estate to fortify themselves in the most astonishing manner. Such a task, which must have taxed the strength of a whole generation at least, would never have been lightly undertaken. There must have been some especially urgent and pressing need to make these free men shift great stone blocks weighing literally millions of tons, with what was undoubtedly most primitive equipment. (For the physical appearance of the Achaeans see Plate 8.)

It should be noted that these fortresses were always situated on quite shallow knolls, so that cattle could be driven into them without difficulty. The stockades inside were provided with a water-supply. Mycenae had only a small enclosure, built by Orestes and in all likelihood reserved as pasturage for the royal horses. Tiryns was better served, and had a cattle-stockade down in the plain, which she probably shared conjointly with Argos. The Achaeans had also set up a large number of fortified outposts, designed to prevent raids on their territory; these were strategically placed, very often in mountain passes. We know of more than thirty such: they only guarded the passes that could be negotiated by chariot, and in Greece these were few and far between. To warriors weighted down by heavy armour[195] the rest of the country was virtually inaccessible. The goatherds could mount their raids at leisure in these mountain fastnesses, and retreat afterwards to positions which, at the time, remained absolutely impregnable.

Cadmus clearly had no intention of running any needless risks. After his magnificent initial successes he set about fortifying Thebes. The result left an indelible impression on the minds of the Greeks. Perhaps because Thebes continued to play a major part in history until the Hellenistic era, perhaps because its famous seven-gated ramparts and its fortress, the Cadmeia, remained standing till the very end, both it and they achieved undying fame throughout the entire Greek world.

Boeotia was at this time the richest area in Greece. Though it did not form the country's heart and nerve-centre, Thebes was nevertheless well placed to reap the advantages of this prosperity. Nor can there be any reasonable doubt that, once Cadmus was safely ensconced in power, neither he nor his descendants had any difficulty in moving from poverty to wealth. The mighty ramparts they could afford to build are tangible proof of that. They certainly became graziers on a large scale, breeding every type of herd then known: their white horses were famous. Wine, too, spread rapidly in Greece, and from the evidence of the amphoras we know that as early as 1300 wine had replaced hydromel at feasts.[196]

But the ideological cleavage remained. However wealthy Thebes became, she was still the symbol of Dionysiac religion, and the followers of the goat persisted in their allegiance, for all her white horses. As Cadmus had rightly foreseen, this handful of Tyrians constituted a redoubtable political force. In the last resort, the cattle-breeders were never to forgive these intruders for having organised the mountain shepherds and goatherds as a coherent force, thus compelling the cities of the plain to surround themselves with their Cyclopean ramparts—a task which called for the most tremendous sustained effort. They finally managed to drive out the Cadmeans; but despite this they themselves succumbed, in the end, to the onslaughts of these mountain-bred fighters, who had remained so much more virile, warlike, and fast-moving than they had. It is this sequence of events which—now all the actors in the drama have taken their places—I propose to follow through.

CHAPTER IV

The Early Dynasties

THE dynasties which were established in Crete and Thebes both began shortly after the invasion of Crete by the Achaeans in 1405, and were a direct result of that invasion. But the situation at Argos, Mycenae and Tiryns was somewhat different, and this discrepancy merits careful study. When Homer had occasion to speak of the Greeks in general, he called them either 'Achaeans' or 'Danaans', without distinction, according to whether his scansion called for a long or a short syllable. The latter term derives from the name of a king of Argos, Danaus, whose statue had, at some very early date,[197] been set up in Delphi—probably during the second-phase period associated with the sacred hive, which we have discussed above. When Cadmus seized Delphi, he must surely have done away with the sacred hive: its connection with the bull-cult was all too obvious, and as a wine-drinking people the Tyrians could not possibly retain it. According to Pausanias[198] the third temple at Delphi was of bronze, which probably means that it was covered with bronze plates[199]—like the Cadmus-Dionysus log mentioned above, and the famous temple at Sparta.[200] It is probable that the ancient statue of Danaus was also destroyed then, *c.* 1360; and it seems more than likely that a memory of this bronze-plated temple underlies the verse of Hesiod according to which the men of this age had brazen houses.[201]

King Danaus must have been a very remarkable character; perhaps, without exaggeration, comparable to Cadmus, whom we have considered in the previous chapter. He organised the bull-worshipping world, just as Cadmus must have organised the goat-worshipping world: and this is perfectly natural when we consider the lapse of time —about two centuries, 1550–1350—which separates the activities of these great Greek Bronze Age pioneers.

All our ancient sources agree in making Danaus come to Argos from Egypt.[202] Now Perseus, whom I have dated *c.* 1360, was the son of Danaë, the last descendant of this illustrious family. Danaë was the

9 A general view of Mycenae

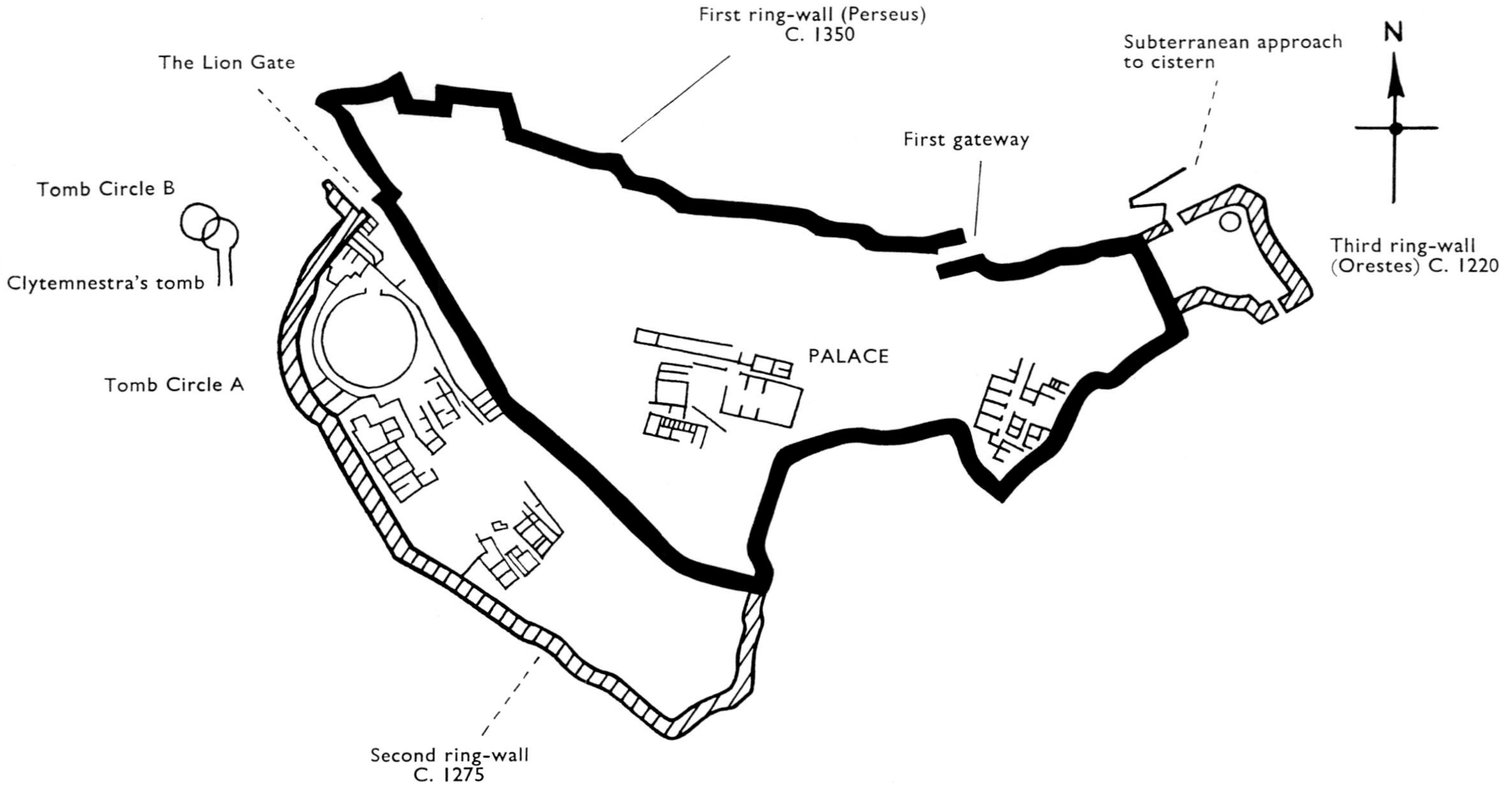

10 Sketch of the ground plan of Mycenae

daughter of Acrisius,[203] himself the great-grandson of Danaus.[204] So early a historian as Hecataeus knew that Perseus's mother was non-Greek, and was called Danâ.[205] This, as we have seen, would put Danaus's *floruit* six generations before Perseus, about the middle of the sixteenth century B.C. We know from our Egyptian sources that it was just about this period (shortly before 1550) that the first Pharaoh of the Eighteenth Dynasty, Amosis the Liberator, succeeded in driving the Hyksos out of Egypt. Now the name 'Hyksos' means 'shepherd'; and we have grounds for supposing that this event and the settlement of the Danaans in Argos were not unconnected.

The tribe of Dan, in fact, is one of the tribes of Israel.[206] It was located somewhere on the Mediterranean coast, where it pillaged passing caravans.[207] When the Philistines reached this coastal area, a series of bloody battles took place. But there is no evidence that the Philistines ever penetrated as far as the Balkans, and to assert that they took part in the battles of the Bronze Age is an all too often repeated anachronism. The Philistines' defeat at Zahi, which effectively checked their advance, took place between the fifth and the eleventh year of the reign of Rameses III, i.e. between 1195 and 1189, or almost a century and a half after the period with which we are concerned. Further, all Philistine pottery comes from Palestine; its style is not a true imitation of Mycenaean ware, but merely derivative. The history of this tribe, then, is wholly restricted to Asia and Egypt.[208]

The story of Samson, on the other hand, is the traditional—if somewhat mythicised—account of how the tribe of Dan came to be expelled. We still have an historical narrative[209] of the wanderings of that part of the tribe which fled northwards, and founded the city of Dan on the site of ancient Leshem.[210] From this time on, Palestine traditionally stretched from Dan to Beersheba. It was in this city of Dan that Jeroboam set up one of his golden calves.[211] The tribe of Dan had certainly taken part in the exodus; and its priests, after the expulsion of the whole clan by the Pharaoh, claimed a line of succession going back to Moses.[212] What is all-important about this story from our point of view is the fact that, throughout the monarchical period, Dan's importance was almost exclusively religious. This stemmed from the tribe's deification of the bull:[213] they had been bull-worshippers from a period which certainly pre-dates the exodus.

The section of the tribe which took part in this exodus was driven out of Egypt about 1550, at the same time as the Hyksos. One branch made its way to the Argolid. There they found the Achaeans, living peacefully in unfortified villages: the countryside was more or less deserted, and the overpopulation which took place two centuries later a very distant prospect indeed. These strangers—whose level of civilisation was far higher than that of the indigenous inhabitants—received a friendly welcome: this is not surprising when we remember the crucial fact that Achaeans and Danaans practised the same religion—that of the bull. The tremendous contribution which these Egyptianised Phoenicians made to the development of Greek culture may very largely explain both their own rise to power, and the sudden efflorescence of local artistic activity after their arrival among the unwarlike, far from xenophobic inhabitants. In all likelihood it was these Dans who brought with them from Egypt the idea of the carved rock-tomb, since such tombs now begin to turn up alongside the traditional shaft-graves. All in all, as I have shown, the history of the Dans runs remarkably parallel to that of the Cadmeans. Bull-worshippers themselves, they contrived—thanks to their more advanced level of civilisation—first to put their Greek fellow votaries on an organised footing, and afterwards to become their leaders. Cadmus's followers did exactly the same thing for the goat-worshippers. But there was one basic difference between them. External circumstances allowed the Dans to stay on for centuries in the Argolid: they became completely Graecised, and were regarded as identical with the Achaeans. The Cadmeans, on the other hand, were forced into war as early as the third generation, and never properly assimilated; in the end the Achaeans drove them out, though for all that they never succeeded in eradicating the deep marks their influence left behind.

The Tell-el-Amarna tablets (which can be dated *c.* 1365 B.C.)[214] refer to a kingdom called Danuna, which is associated with Ugarit. This probably represents the habitat of the bull-worshipping group which had left Egypt and sought refuge in Syria. Once again, the Minoans and Achaeans of Ugarit professed the same religion as these refugees. It seems very likely, therefore, that our Danaans in the Argolid, the Danuna of Syria, the Palestinian tribe of Dan and the clan of the same name which took part in the exodus are, ultimately, all branches of the same central stem, branches united from the beginning by a common religion, the bull-cult. This would have the advantage of explaining one fact which at first sight looks somewhat odd. Perseus, the last of the Danaans and the first architect of Mycenae, married—according to tradition[215]—Andromeda, herself a princess of Joppa (the modern Jaffa). This begins to look a little less strange when we recall that the tribe of Dan's immediate neighbour was that of Joppa.[216] Long sundered in both time and space, their natural tribal and religious affinities must now have come into play once more, demonstrating the primordial power they exerted—which, indeed, never lost its force throughout the whole of the Bronze Age. Apollodorus[217] has preserved a tradition that Perseus exchanged Argos against Tiryns, Midea, and Mycenae, which he proceeded to fortify. Argos he is supposed to have handed over to Megapenthes: the reason being that he had inadvertently killed his own grandfather Acrisius—an oracle had predicted Acrisius's death—and as a result of this accident he no longer wished to return to Argos. The story is somewhat confused, but Apollodorus has a habit of getting the separate threads of his narrative tangled. In the last resort this need not concern us here, however: the only point of any importance to us is the fact that the Cyclopean defences of the cities in the Argolid were—at least in their initial stage—linked with with the name of Perseus. And if we examine all these colossal fortification-works, from Dendra-Midea to Asine, we are forced to concede that Perseus was one of the greatest builders of all time.

His Danaan ancestors had known how to keep the Argolid in a state of peace and rising prosperity. Perhaps some of them—till we put them in our museums—slept their last sleep in the shaft-graves of Circles A and B at Mycenae, or the rock-tombs of Argive Larissa, or perhaps at Dendra: who will ever know? The overpopulation which this admirable stewardship brought about may have driven the Danaans to fortify their cities, but it likewise furnished them with the abundant supply of labour which such fortifications required. The Cyclopean architects were there, ready to hand. Perseus—who was also a great organiser and administrator—concluded the immense task which circumstances had forced upon him in less than thirty years: it is something very like a miracle.

Here we must consider an incident which had some far-reaching consequences: the fortification of Tiryns was to bring a whole trail of unforeseen events in its wake. All this reorganisation that Perseus had undertaken was, basically, designed to give one section of the population the means to defend themselves against another, which since its own organisation by Cadmus had been becoming more and more aggressive. This new system devised by Perseus was to culminate in the complex and ingenious administration which the Pylos tablets reveal to us. It undoubtedly was associated, in the first instance, with the redeployment of the open villages round these new fortresses, which could offer refuge to both the inhabitants and their cattle in the event of raids by mountain herdsmen against the rich plain-dwellers. The close proximity of the Argive fortresses one to another shows how vital a factor it was to be within easy reach of one's refuge-point. This is the 'synoecismus' attributed to Theseus in Athens—probably wrongly, since it appears to have taken place somewhat later.

This new way of life in the plains, centred on villages built under the shadow of some megalithic palace, could not but emphasise yet more distinctly the way the population had split into two alien groups. The goat-worshipping followers of Dionysus for various reasons refused (if they were ever invited) to come down and live beneath the walls of strongholds built by the bull-worshipping followers of Zagreus; so these goatherds and sheep-breeders henceforth became, *ipso facto*, suspect—men liable to launch murderous raids against the inhabitants of the new fortresses.

There was a certain nobleman called Amphitryon, who lived near Tiryns and claimed that his ancestors had come 'out of Egypt'[218]—which meant, probably, that he was descended from one of Danaus's original companions. He had married a wife of rare beauty, whose name was Alcmene. It seems likely that his family had come down in the world, and that he was a breeder of sheep or goats, since—as his subsequent career shows—he was, beyond a doubt, to be numbered amongst the goat-worshippers. Had his brilliant marriage perhaps gone to his head? Whatever the reason, the fact remains that he coveted his father-in-law's herds of oxen, quarrelled with him over them, and finally killed him.[219] After this domestic drama he preferred—for reasons that we will detail later—not to come and dwell under the protection of the walls that Perseus was then having built at Tiryns; instead, 'leaving his native land he came to Thebes,[220] as a suppliant before the shield-bearing Cadmeans'.[221] Thebes, of course, was the capital of the Dionysiac cult: Amphitryon was welcomed with open arms (a fact that shows what his religion was), and it was here, in Boeotia, that Alcmene gave birth to twin boys.[222] But these twins had been conceived in a decidedly uncommon fashion, for Alcmene, during the same night, had intercourse with both Amphitryon and Zeus, so that one of her children, Heracles, was begotten by Zeus, and the other, Iphicles, by Amphitryon.[223] According to our synoptic chronological table, this extraordinary conception (which was to have a thousand untold consequences) means that the twins must have been born in 1320.

11a The walls of Midea

b The entrance gate at Midea

12 Two views of the remains of the Mycenaean acropolis of Athens

But the birth of these children was only one among several happenings which were destined to weigh heavily on the subsequent history of Thebes and Mycenae alike. About 1340, a very wealthy stranger named Pelops arrived in Elis from Asia Minor.[224] Tradition[225] has it that in his retinue were the first Greeks who called themselves 'Achaeans', their place of origin being Thessaly. Because of Pelops's brilliant destiny, it is said, this appellation became more widespread as time went on, and was used in the end to designate all Bronze Age Greeks whatsoever.

Be that as it may, Pelops won the hand of Hippodameia, daughter of Oenomaus, the King of Elis:[226] this he did thanks to his victory in a famous chariot race, commemorated by the magnificent sculptured frieze on one of the pediments of the great temple at Olympia. The union of Pelops and Hippodameia was a fertile one. They had four children; two daughters, Nicippe, who was probably the eldest, and her sister Lysidice, and then, in that order, two boys, Atreus and Thyestes.[227]

Nicippe, who must have been about the most eligible bride of her age, married Sthenelus, son and heir to the great king of Mycenae, Tiryns and Midea,[228] Perseus the Danaan. Perseus lived until 1315, at which date Sthenelus succeeded him; but in 1320,[229] when Sthenelus was still only the heir apparent, he found that his wife Nicippe was pregnant (with a son, as it turned out, the future Eurystheus) in Mycenae, at the same time as Alcmene was expecting her famous double-sired twins in Thebes. It goes without saying that, as far as all bull-worshippers were concerned, Alcmene and Amphitryon could be regarded as nothing but the most abominable Dionysiac renegades. The Achaean landed gentry were outraged: it was rather as though the eighteenth-century Duke of Buckingham had suddenly announced his conversion to Islam.

This explains why, up on Olympus, 'ox-eyed' [*boôpis*] Hera (who detested everything connected, however tenuously, with the goat) decided to play an extremely nasty trick on this faithless, lawless couple. She knew that one of the twins Alcmene was expecting had been sired by Zeus, and this fact merely exacerbated her anger: such a divine pedigree would open up a number of possibilities for Heracles—especially as regards the throne of Tiryns, which lay, after all, only a few miles from Mycenae. Furthermore she knew that, in the normal course of events, Alcmene was due to give birth some two months before Nicippe. She therefore made Zeus swear that the first-born male child of these two *accouchements*, whoever its mother, should succeed to the throne of Mycenae. She then caused Nicippe to go into labour first, at seven months; and so, on the death of his father Sthenelus in 1290, it was Eurystheus who became King of Mycenae[230] and Heracles who afterwards had to perform, at his bidding, the famous Labours.[231] These symbolise, very aptly, the haughty arrogance of the wealthy Achaeans, with their herds of cattle and their fortress-palaces, towards those of their countrymen who lived on the uplands and kept goats. (It is interesting to note that the first six Labours are located in the Peloponnese. The remainder move to Crete, Thrace, Spain, and, finally, the next world.[232]) We know that in the district of Thebes only goats were sacrificed,[233] a fact which shows us both the local popularity of the Dionysiac cult, and the position Thebes occupied as the 'goatherds' capital', despite its geographical position in lush Boeotia, where cattle-breeding must certainly have predominated. The fact that the Cadmeans could collect *some* supporters from every part of Greece suggests a degree of conscious political thought behind the schism.

But the central fact to remember, in this long and complicated story, is that the twins, Heracles and Iphicles, were born at Thebes of *émigrés* from Tiryns more or less at the same time as Eurystheus, child of Sthenelus and Nicippe, was born at Mycenae. This correlation is vital for dating the Mycenaean dynasty and hence the whole history of Greece in the late Bronze Age. Let me repeat also that in placing the birth of Heracles about 1320 we agree with the testimony of Herodotus, who supposes him to have lived *circa* 1300.[234]

It is hard to disentangle any specific facts from the myth of Heracles: here legend has accumulated too thickly. Do the twelve Labours conceal some genuine historical incident? Today, alas, it would seem impossible to tell. Heracles was the son of an *émigré*, perhaps of an exile. He may well have inherited certain rights to the sovereignty of Tiryns; but his rivalry with Eurystheus[235] turned to his disadvantage, and he probably ended his own life in exile (there are many contradictory traditions about this), in a Greek world that was beginning to settle down under the rule of the first dynasties which—through fear of internal rebellion—the Achaeans had come to accept. These dynasties did not recognise Heracles' ascendancy, and, having first compelled him to serve them by force (the twelve Labours), latterly drove him into exile, perhaps as far afield as Scythia. This was a Dionysiac country, and here Heracles is supposed to have married a woman who was a fish from the waist down. He had three sons by her, who all inherited their mother's oddity: today, two and a half millennia later, we can still see

13a An Achaean nobleman from Mycenae driving out to war

b An Achaean nobleman from Tiryns driving out to war

14 An Achaean nobleman from Corinth driving out to war

them on the pediment of an archaic Athenian temple, watching their father's attempts to seize the sacred tripod.

What is beyond doubt is that Heracles became a rallying-point for the whole anti-Zagreus faction: his most important temple was set up in Tyre[236]—home of Cadmus, of wine, of the sacred goat; a fact which says much for Heracles' natural affinities. Furthermore, the destruction of the civilisation associated with the bull was known to history as 'the return of the Heraclidae (or sons of Heracles)', and not as 'the Dorian invasion'—a phenomenon of which the ancient world seems to have remained consistently ignorant.

By his second wife, Deianira, Heracles had a son called Hyllus,[237] who played an important part in these events, and to whom I shall return presently. He also had a nephew, Iolaus, the son of his twin brother Iphicles, who took part, about 1285, in a raid organised by one of Cadmus's descendants—probably Laïus, though it could, just, have been Oedipus—against the still unfortified territory of Attica.

Perseus had died about 1315, and was succeeded by his son Sthenelus. Sthenelus himself died about 1290, and the next to occupy the throne of Mycenae was Eurystheus—the same Eurystheus whose birth Hera had induced prematurely in order to secure him his crown, who was the exact contemporary of Heracles and Iphicles. The Cadmean raid into Attica must have alarmed this scion of the House of Perseus: the cult of Dionysus was gaining ground in the most disturbing way, and these goatherds had become an aggressive menace. Now that the Peloponnese was fortified, bristling with megalithic fortresses that could keep the local malcontents at bay, one might safely enough undertake an expedition. So the King of Mycenae—probably for the first time in history—decided to make a personal intervention. At the head of his troops (who were, we may surmise, mounted in their famous chariots) he rode into Attica and fought a battle with the Cadmeans. Misfortune overtook him: he was struck down, and Iolaus, the nephew of Heracles, personally decapitated him.[238]

The violent death of Eurystheus, who was probably, at the time, the most important single person in the Achaean world, must have produced vast repercussions throughout Greece. It was a stern warning of the fate which lay in store for the cattle-graziers if they failed to organise themselves properly. The King of Mycenae had been killed by these presumptuous *émigré* Syrians, assisted by bands of goatherds: everyone realised, instantly, how imminent was the danger that threatened the rich plainland. Reactions to the event followed soon enough.

To begin with, there was trouble at Mycenae. The first palace, built by Perseus, was burnt down, and the same thing happened at Tiryns. The Perseid-Danaan dynasty was ousted from the throne in favour of the House of Pelops, as represented by Atreus—who was blood-brother to Nicippe, the mother of the lately dead King Eurystheus.

Work began in Attica, at feverish speed: and soon[239] the first Cyclopean wall encircled the hitherto undefended Acropolis.[240] Now any Theban invaders could be met and held. But the most violent reaction was in Boeotia itself. Orchomenus built its citadel almost at insolent Thebes' very gates; and, most important of all, the Boeotians undertook a pioneer essay in collective defence—a method which was to be adopted throughout the Achaean world, and give it, for two centuries, an uncontested supremacy. The graziers who lived round the rich marshlands of Lake Copaïs built what is probably the most gigantic war-machine of all time. On a long, low-lying, but nevertheless sheer-sided promontory, which in those days must have been almost completely surrounded by water, they erected the colossal ring-wall of Gla,[241] more than three thousand yards in circumference, with two palaces inside it, not to mention store-rooms and inner dividing walls,

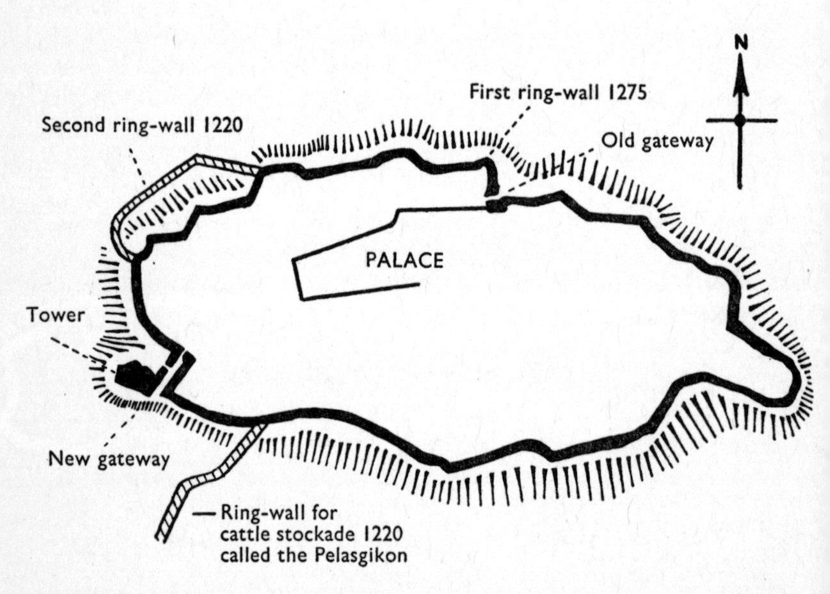

Sketch of the ground plan of the Mycenaean Acropolis of Athens. (See Plate 12.)

15a A view of a part of the walls of Gla

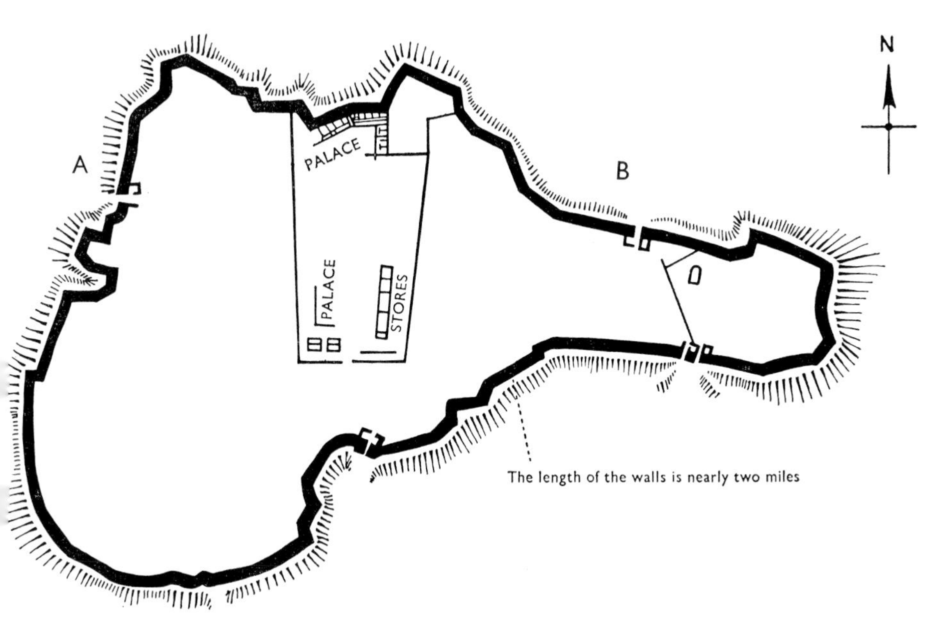

b Sketch of the ground plan of Gla

16 Views of the gateways at Gla shown at A (above) and B on the plan overleaf

MYCENAE

1405 The Palace of Cnossos burnt down by Achaean Invaders (first fire)

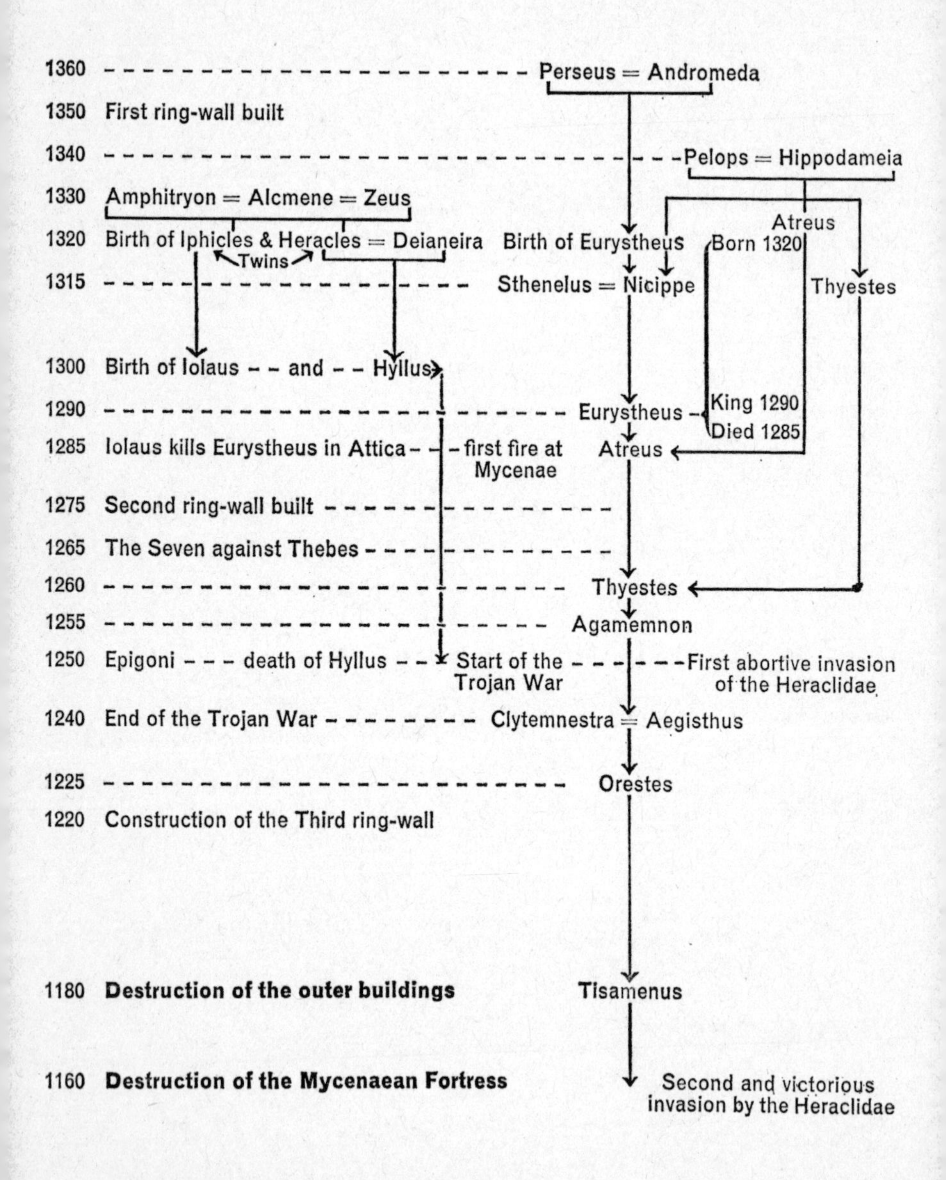

1100 Cnossos burnt for the second time

THEBES

1405 Palace of Cnossos burnt down by Achaean Invaders (first fire)

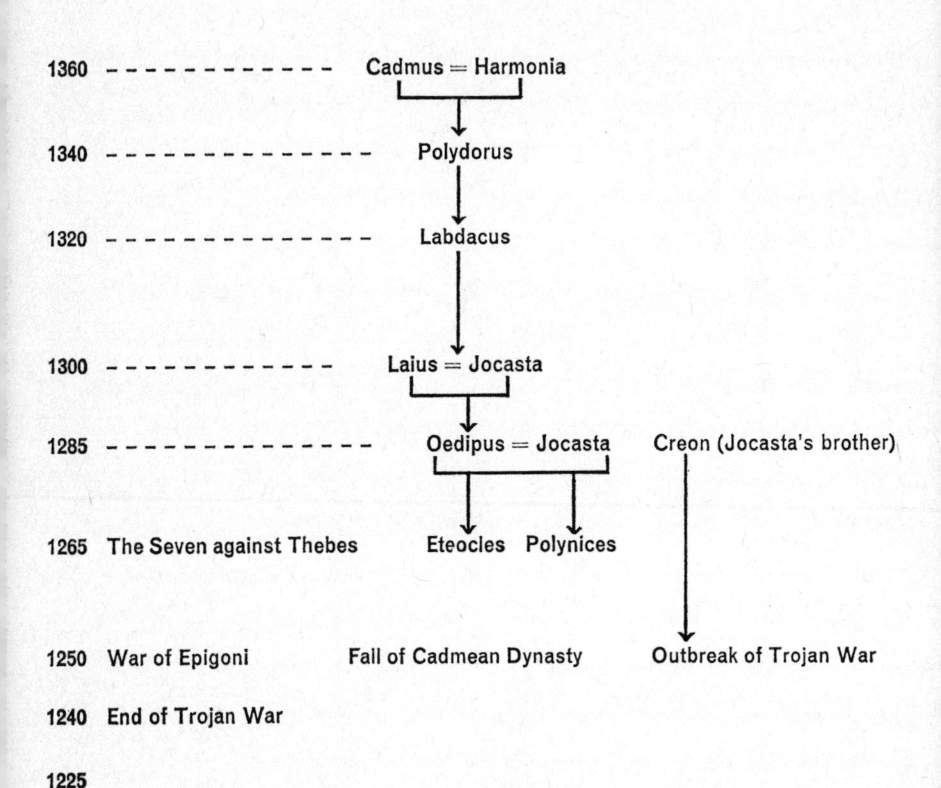

1240 End of Trojan War

1225

1180 Destruction of Pylos

1160 Destruction of Mycenae

1100 Second burning of Cnossos

CRETE

1405 **Palace of Cnossos burnt down by Achaean Invaders (first fire)**

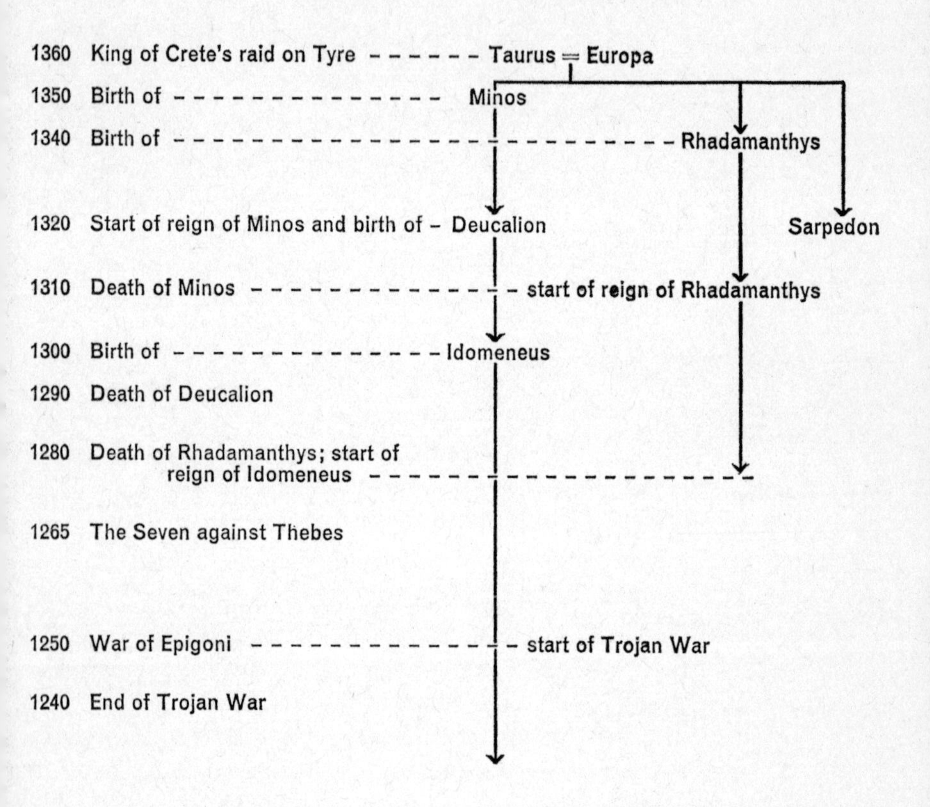

1180 **Destruction of Pylos**

1160 **Destruction of Mycenae**

1100 **Cnossos burnt for the second time**

the latter perhaps to keep cattle and horses separate.[242] Gla's indisputably co-operative character is of very great interest: it shows the awakening of that feeling of solidarity which, by uniting the Achaean landowners as a class, enabled them to accomplish those exploits that were to resound through history, and which culminated in the Trojan War.

In Crete, the death of Eurystheus had one rather curious consequence: it brought about the only attempt at planned colonisation [243]which we hear of in Achaean history, and we can only regret that other régimes struggling to combat overpopulation did not follow this lead. It was, surely, a more efficacious remedy than the erection of Cyclopean ramparts as a defence against malcontents. Now in 1285 or thereabouts Rhadamanthus was still on the Cretan throne; there was not, it has been argued, much love lost between him and his younger brother Sarpedon. After over a century of prudent Achaean administration, which had contrived to keep the great island free from embroilment of any sort, we can be pretty sure that the effects of overpopulation—so acutely distressing in 1100, to judge from the Linear B tablets—must have already begun to make people uncomfortably aware of their existence, as on the mainland. Sarpedon[244] possessed the palace of Milatus in Crete; Rhadamanthus exiled him, together with a number of his followers—all, as we shall see, goat-worshippers—and sent them to colonise Miletus on the Ionian coast.[245] He thus solved the overpopulation problem for a century: not too bad an achievement, all things considered. He may well have been driven to this measure for the reason I have outlined above—that is, the impossibility of erecting in Crete those Cyclopean defences which the mainland princes put up to protect themselves against raids by the herdsmen.

The religious allegiance of Sarpedon's followers is indicated by the odd fact that, whereas the contingents from Cretan Milatus, under Idomeneus's command, fought beside Agamemnon[246] in the Trojan War, the forces raised by the synonymous city in Asia Minor were, on the contrary, allied to the Dionysus-worshipping Trojans.[247] Rancour and prejudice were already deeply engrained, and what today we refer to as the class struggle must have been acute. Sarpedon probably took only men with him; according to Herodotus they all married Carian wives, which explains why Homer says that two generations later the inhabitants of Ionian Miletus were Carians, who spoke a barbarous (i.e. non-Greek) language. Herodotus also states that the Termilae of Lycia believed themselves to be descended from the colonists who had accompanied Sarpedon to Asia Minor.[248] The distribution of Lycian inscriptions in the south-west corner of Asia Minor, opposite Crete, supports this tradition; and Herodotus's claim that the Lycians referred to themselves as Termilae finds confirmation in the inscriptions themselves,[249] where the name 'Termilae' is mentioned.[250]

These measures, by and large, proved efficacious enough: the hour of the herdsmen's revenge had not yet struck—especially since Atreus showed himself a more than capable ruler. He was, indeed, a very great sovereign, after the model of Perseus. He made considerable improvements to Mycenae's defence system, chiefly by extending the ring-wall so as to bring Grave Circle A within the ramparts, and replacing the original entrance by the Lion Gate.[251] At Tiryns he constructed the great cattle stockade which, together with that of Argos, should have sufficed to protect all the heavy livestock from raids by mountain herdsmen.

Having thus put the country on a proper defence footing, Atreus appealed to the other Greek princes' spirit of co-operation—a spirit which had already manifested its existence at Gla—and the Achaeans combined to bar the Isthmus with a Cyclopean wall.[252] This was an undertaking the scope of which really defies the imagination—yet it must have been accomplished in an amazingly brief span of time, somewhere between 1280 and 1270. It testifies in the most eloquent manner both to the abundance of ready labour and to the imminence of the danger it sought to avert. One is tempted to ask oneself whether the Cadmean threat was sufficient to justify this superhuman effort, or whether the infiltration of hostile tribes, which it was so vital to halt at all costs, had not in fact already begun. I shall discuss this point in more detail presently.

Having thus organised Greece as he thought fit, Atreus now turned his attention to Thebes. (In the interim he probably constructed his own tomb, known today as the 'Treasury of Atreus', which dates from this period.) No one had forgotten that it was the Thebans who had killed his predecessor,[253] or that it was they who were behind the constant rebellious activities of the small graziers. Atreus launched his first campaign against the goat-worshippers' capital itself.[254] It was an important undertaking, and the scale on which the expedition was planned may be gauged by the fact that even Cretans took part in it. In those days the journey from Cnossos to Thebes was long and hazardous. Moreover there must have existed an anti-Cadmean party in Thebes itself—symbolised traditionally by the fact that Polynices, one of Oedipus's two sons, fought with the Argive contingent. (There are numerous legends to account for his defection.)

This expedition, the first organised Greek campaign known to history, struck men's imaginations very vividly, and remained famous in after time as the expedition of the Seven against Thebes.[255] But the walls of Thebes were strong, and—as I have already suggested—Achaean methods of warfare far from efficient. Perhaps, in this first combined operation, the planning, too, was somewhat lacking. At all events, according to tradition, all seven leaders were killed in the assaults on the various gates; after a brief campaign the expedition fizzled out and the Achaean forces were disbanded. In this first trial of strength between the Goat and the Bull, the Goat had emerged victorious. The campaign must have been fought somewhere about 1265; and the humiliation experienced by the Achaean warriors—whom Homer depicts as inveterate braggarts—must have been agonising.

Shortly after this defeat, *c.* 1260, Atreus died, and was succeeded by his brother Thyestes. Thyestes's reign must have been very short: even supposing him to have been ten years younger than his elder sister Nicippe, he would be well advanced in age by now. Then, about 1255, it was the turn of Agamemnon, Atreus's son, to ascend the throne of Mycenae.

The tension between rich and poor, which a steady increase in population could only serve to exacerbate, must have become a good deal worse by now, with Bull and Goat opposed more implacably than ever; for Agamemnon's first concern was to renew operations against Thebes, that hotbed of Dionysiac dissidents, all of whom were, apparently, in a permanent state of quasi-revolt. But now, thanks both to their fortifications and to the wall barring the Isthmus, the bull-worshippers had acquired a certain degree of mobility. Perhaps, too, they had learnt from the errors of the past, and the experience gained during the first campaign of the 'Seven' now proceeded to bear fruit.[256] So it came about that, shortly before 1250, Agamemnon organised the expedition known as that of the Epigoni,[257] and the Achaeans once more besieged the Cadmeans in their seven-gated city. At this point Thebes had no leader worthy of the name. Cadmus's direct line was extinct; the tragedy of Oedipus had decimated the royal family. The present ruler was an elderly brother of Jocasta's named Creon, who himself had no heir. Resistance lasted only a short while, and then Thebes fell. Though captured, she was not, it seems, destroyed. Her enormous fortifications endured until the Hellenistic era: in the Bronze Age men built to last for ever. The Cadmeans—that is, as we shall see, those Boeotians descended from Syrian immigrants—were permitted to withdraw to Illyria,[258] and for six centuries Thebes vanished from history.

This is the point at which we must consider the most interesting story of Hyllus, Heracles's son by Deianeira; a story which Herodotus recounts in some detail.[259] From Herodotus's narrative it appears that after the capture of Thebes by the Achaeans, Hyllus attempted to lead the 'Heraclidae' (by which is probably meant those Peloponnesian sheep or goat breeders who, for one reason or another, had sought refuge in Thebes) into 'the lands of their fathers', which are specified as being the region round about Tiryns. But when he reached the wall spanning the Isthmus, Hyllus came up against a combined force of Tegeans, Achaeans and Ionians;[260] from which we may conclude that his enemies had prior intelligence of his movements. In the end he was killed by Echemus the Tegean; and it was then, about 1250, that the Heraclidae (according to tradition) swore to abstain for a century from all incursions into the Peloponnese. It is true, in fact, that their next expedition—which was crowned with success—can be dated to a period shortly after 1160. It was, as I have suggested above, the lapse of time between these two events which gave rise to the myth reported by Herodotus—which he presents as part of the speech delivered by the Tegean herald before the battle of Plataea.

The Athenian herald's reply on the same occasion contains one important detail concerning the history of our period. According to this spokesman for the army of Attica, Theseus's descendants had defended the Heraclidae in 1285, but twenty years later had attacked the Cadmeans in order to recover the bodies of the seven slain chieftains, and give them burial at Eleusis.[261] The story, as the Athenian herald tells it, looks somewhat inconsistent; but the careful way in which Herodotus distinguishes between 'Cadmeans' and 'Heraclidae' has some underlying significance. The distinction must have been a traditional one, and whichever version of the myth one prefers, it is still there. The 'Cadmeans' can only have been the descendants of Cadmus's original Tyrian followers, resident now for four generations, and still not assimilated to the Greeks; whereas the 'Heraclidae' were descended from those Achaeans who had come with Amphitryon, about 1330, from the neighbourhood of Tiryns in the Peloponnese. The ties binding the latter to the Cadmeans of seven-gated Thebes were clearly not racial, and must, in fact, as I demonstrated earlier, have been of a religious or, more specifically, a Dionysiac nature.[262]

But the story Herodotus tells us throws unexpected light on another side of the question, which is crucially important if we are to understand the subsequent course events took. The internal situation (once again, we find no evidence at this point for any enemies beyond the frontiers) must indeed have been critical to make Atreus undertake the immense modifications which he carried out on the fortresses of Tiryns and Mycenae, and for Gla, Orchomenus and Athens all to have been rebuilt from scratch during the same period. But we may still legitimately ask whether the very considerable joint effort to which the Achaean world committed itself—two major campaigns against Thebes, and, above all, the construction of that gigantic wall, nearly four miles long, right across the Isthmus—could possibly be justified in the year 1250 by the might of Cadmean Thebes, which, under the aged Creon, had surely reached a state of complete decadence?

The answer, I feel, is in the negative; and though the wall proved invaluable for halting Hyllus and his followers, Herodotus's text nowhere suggests that it was equally indispensable as a bulwark against the invasion of the Heraclidae. The message Hyllus sent to the enemy commander (suggesting that in the interests of saving men's lives the conflict should be decided by a duel between two chieftains) reveals, *au fond*, how loath Achaeans were, during this period, to fight against other Achaeans. This was, moreover, the secret of their prosperity as an empire—and the cause of their steadily increasing overpopulation. It would seem, then, that we must look elsewhere for the reason *why* a wall designed to ensure the collective defence of the Peloponnese should have been built between 1280 and 1270. The only possible danger, apart from Thebes, that can have been threatening the Peloponnesians was the progressive infiltration of elements hostile to the cattle-graziers—elements which in all probability came from Asia Minor.

As we have seen above[263] the magnificent city of Troy VI had been destroyed about the year 1300 by a violent earthquake; by the time with which we are now concerned, *circa* 1250, it had been replaced by an unpretentious settlement, patched together piecemeal fashion amid the ruins of the powerful city which Homer's poems still anachronistically commemorate. The Trojans had always been small stock graziers: this is shown by both their weaving industry and the animal bones found in the ruins of their settlements. The catastrophe of 1300 had ruined the country, as the total collapse of her foreign trade makes clear; but her natural affinities had always been with the Aegean rather than the Asiatic world, and when, in the anarchic aftermath of destruction, certain groups decided to emigrate in search of better conditions elsewhere, it was by common consent to mainland Greece that they set out. Thebes, the small stock-breeder's natural spiritual centre, drew them inevitably, like a magnet. From there it was easy enough to drive their flocks down to the Isthmus, and then fan out into Arcadia and the mountain ranges which criss-cross the whole of the Peloponnese. This migratory movement must have been a large-scale affair, and was bound to constitute a grave danger for the wealthy landowners in the plains. It is the only possible explanation of the tremendous concerted effort they made to bar the Isthmus: the Cyclopean wall they built was the biggest project of its kind ever undertaken, Bronze Age Greece's Great Wall of China.

According to Herodotus,[264] the Cadmeans—that is to say, those Boeotians who were of Syrian descent—withdrew to southern Illyria after their defeat at the hands of the Epigoni; the Heraclidae were checked at the Isthmus; and it was probably about this time that the Dorians[265] first began to threaten the defences of the Peloponnese. The complicated tribulations which this tribe endured indicate that its warriors were few in number,[266] and could, on their own, have been made to move on elsewhere without much trouble. But the Dorians, clearly, were not on their own: the defensive steps taken by the Achaean world testify eloquently to the seriousness of the invasion threat during this period.

The Dorians gave their name to the small canton of Doris, situated near Mount Oeta;[267] very probably this happened after the fall of Thebes, when the Cadmeans drove them southwards, opening the way for their own retreat to Illyria. Tradition has it that some of them actually reached Crete by the direct sea route.[268] It might perhaps be those small groups to which Herodotus refers[269] that gave rise to the lines in the *Odyssey* stating that Crete was inhabited, in Odysseus's day, by Eteo-Cretans, Cydonians, Dorians and Pelasgians.[270] Ethnographical statements in the *Odyssey* are, obviously, to be regarded with more than usual suspicion when their immediate context is a collection of old wives' tales;[271] but here they are not altogether absurd if we assume—which is at least credible—that they refer to small scattered groups which did not, as yet, constitute a political threat in what was after all a very large island.

By taking these various factors into account we can perhaps get a clearer understanding of the acute anxiety which, about the mid-

17 Two views of the archaeological excavations at Pylos (the picture above shows the bathroom in which the bath and the system for supplying hot and cold running water are clearly visible)

18 The suit of armour found at Dendra

thirteenth century, affected the wealthier Achaeans. Though they were established very comfortably in their luxurious palaces, they were, by and large, dependent for a livelihood on their herds of cattle and horses—both very vulnerable assets. Furthermore, faced with steadily increasing hostility from the mountain herdsmen—a state of affairs which was now going from bad to worse—they were obliged to ration the products of their as yet undeveloped agriculture most severely: especially since the mountain uplands were more or less inaccessible to these noble warriors, with their chariots and their prohibitively heavy armour, such as that recently discovered at Dendra.[272]

The war of 'the Seven', the expedition of the Epigoni, the construction of Gla and the Isthmus wall had probably demonstrated to the Achaeans just how effective communal enterprise could be. As soon as the power of the Cadmeans had been broken, once and for all, they decided—under Agamemnon's leadership—to strike hard at the root of their troubles, destroy them at source. They would mount a great expedition into Asia Minor, where these dangerous nomadic goatherds came from, and raze Troy to the ground, since it formed the rallying-point for all such rapacious marauders.[273] Better still, they would wipe out this whole accursed race from the face of the earth. 'Let none of them escape death at our hands,' Agamemnon exclaims, 'neither the fugitive nor the child yet in its mother's womb; let the whole population of Ilium perish, unmourned, and leaving no trace behind'.[274] This could scarcely be more explicit. The Achaeans did in fact achieve, by and large, the racial extermination at which they aimed; the bucchero ware of Troy VIIb2 indicates the arrival of new inhabitants. Trojans, as such, ceased to exist.[275]

As for the story of the rape of Helen, Helen herself does not appear to have been Greek in origin, and this trumpery poetic excuse looks as if it was borrowed from the Semitic poem *Keret*. In any case there was an alternative tradition, alluded to in Stesichorus's[276] famous palinode and by Euripides,[277] according to which Helen never went any farther than Egypt. It was the influence of the Semitic *Keret* poems (which originated in the Ugarit area and were written in the cuneiform Canaanite alphabet) that prevailed on the *Iliad*[278] and the *Odyssey*[279] to make Helen actually reach Troy. Did this Near Eastern influence on Greek epic poetry perhaps go back to the thirteenth century, when the Mycenaeans had a trading-post at Ugarit? Or was it the Phoenicians who, by means of their alphabet, passed on these Ugarit poems which are also very closely linked with the Old Testament) to the

Greeks of the eighth century? Today it is still impossible to answer this question; but no doubt the increasingly close attention scholars are paying to Oriental sources for European literature will, ultimately, furnish us with the key to the problem.[280]

Preparations for the great expedition which Agamemnon was to lead began at once. The Greek world had never seen anything remotely like it, and this adventure—which lasted for no less than ten years—left so profound an impression on men's minds that the memory of it endured generation after generation. All the followers of the Bull, nobles and vassals alike, were assembled for this assault on the Goat's stronghold. The roll of contingents which Homer has left us demonstrates what cohesive unity (appearances notwithstanding) the Achaean empire possessed, and how many barons Agamemnon could muster for such an enterprise.

Naturally enough, no Theban contingent is to be found taking part in this struggle, on one side or the other; and after the victory of the Epigoni their absence is not to be wondered at. But we do find a Heraclid, Tlepolemus, fighting for Zagreus against Dionysus.[281] Homer—obviously conscious of this anomaly—goes carefully out of his way to explain it, in the following manner.[282] Tlepolemus, the son of Heracles and Astyoche, had been forced to flee the country because he had killed his father's aged uncle, Licymnius.[283] 'Straightway then he fitted out ships, and gathered a strong force aboard them, and put to sea; for the other sons and grandsons of the mighty Heracles uttered parlous threats against him. So, by a wandering course, and enduring many hardships, he came at last to Rhodes; and there he and his followers dwelt, in three tribes, and were beloved of Zeus. . . .'[284] What Homer means by this, clearly, is that they were converted from the cult of Dionysus to that of Zagreus: they changed their fertility myth. Zeus, furthermore, recompensed them by endowing them with great wealth, which made it possible for them to break into the very exclusive circle of the Achaean nobility.

It is possible to trace Tlepolemus's connection with the Perseid dynasty rather more precisely: this suggests a possible explanation not only for Tlepolemus's own flight to Rhodes, but also for that of Amphitryon to Thebes. In point of fact Perseus had other children by Andromeda apart from Sthenelus, among them Electryon.[265] Electryon married Lysidice, a daughter of Pelops,[286] and thus sister to Nicippe, Sthenelus's wife. In other words, the two sons of Perseus married the two daughters of Pelops. By his wife Lysidice Electryon had a legitimate daughter, Alcmene; and by a Phrygian concubine named Midea[287] he had a bastard son, Licymnius.

Alcmene, as I mentioned earlier, married Amphitryon, who killed his father-in-law Electryon as the result of a quarrel over the Perseid's herds of cattle. Amphitryon's act was clearly a most serious offence, since Electryon was a claimant in the direct line to the throne of Mycenae. It seems, therefore, a reasonable assumption that after this murder Amphitryon was forced to flee with his wife Alcmene to Thebes—

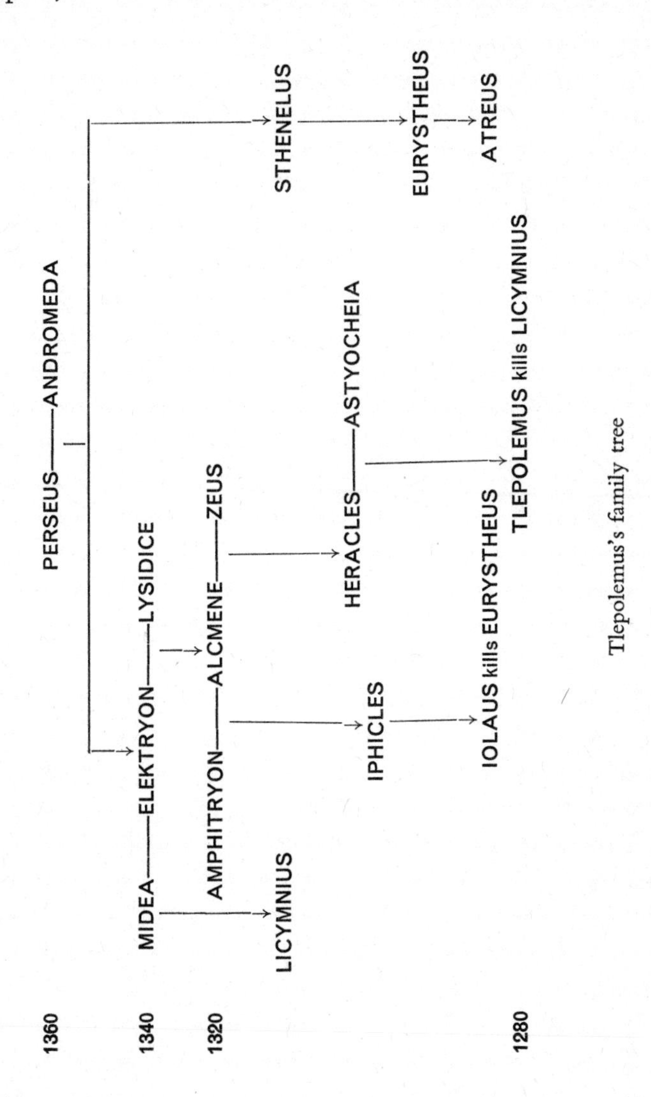

Tlepolemus's family tree

very probably taking with him the riches he had filched from his wife's family. Alcmene's half-brother, Licymnius, being reduced to poverty by this theft, was probably left with no alternative but to throw in his lot with the Peloponnesian goatherds—most of whom were, in fact, cattle-graziers who had lost their inheritance.

Alcmene, as we saw, subsequently bore Heracles to Zeus; and Heracles in his turn sired a bastard, Tlepolemus, on his concubine Astyocheia.[288] This Tlepolemus was, therefore, the great-nephew of Licymnius [see genealogical chart on p. 79]. When Eurystheus was killed, in 1285, Licymnius found himself the last surviving member of the House of Perseus; and when Atreus robbed him of his Mycenaean throne, which now passed to the dynasty of the Pelopidae, it is only natural to suppose that Licymnius aligned himself with the group opposed to the new régime—i.e. with the followers of Dionysus. His birth and the very special position he occupied must have made the Cadmeans, as leaders and organisers of the goat-worshipping faction, treat him with great respect: his political value to them was enormous.

It seems likely that about 1280 Tlepolemus accidentally killed his great-uncle Licymnius: the version of the story adopted by Pindar seems not to have won credence in antiquity. But it is, nevertheless, possible that this second murder might be regarded as in some sense a sequel to the more or less parallel killing of Electryon by Amphitryon—which must have left much hatred and bitterness behind it.

Be that as it may, and despite the fact that Licymnius and Tlepolemus belonged to the same party, it was against Tlepolemus that the clan's desire for vengeance unleashed itself. In fact, though Tlepolemus was one of Heracles's innumerable sons, he nevertheless remained unimportant by reason of his illegitimacy; whereas Licymnius, as the last of the Perseids (who had, moreover, changed his allegiance to Dionysus) represented a valuable political weapon, and one which might prove more than useful to the Mycenaean refugees living in Thebes, as an extra argument to reinforce their endless claims. Furious at finding themselves thus robbed of so precious a trump card, the Heraclidae turned against Tlepolemus,[289] forcing him and his companions to take hasty flight to Rhodes.

The Achaeans in Rhodes, moreover, have a very special interest for us when we are establishing the dates of those events which concern us here. They were at loggerheads with the Hittite emperors, and the latter's archives have yielded duplicate copies of a lengthy correspondence between them and the Rhodian overlords. The people of Rhodes must have called themselves Akhaiwoi, and the Hittites referred to their island by the cognate appellation of Akhijawa. This correspondence extends right through the first half of the thirteenth century B.C., and deserves to be correlated far more closely than has hitherto been the case with other events in the Achaean world.[290]

Apart from Tlepolemus,[291] Homer refers only to two other little-known Heraclidae who fought on Agamemnon's side,[292] and we do not know what their motives may have been. On the other hand, 'rocky Pytho'[293] and 'divine Crisa'[294] appear side by side amongst the contingent from Phocis, which is a modest enough force: eight localities, and no more than forty ships between them. This shows that after the fall of the Cadmeans, Phocis had once more allied itself with those orthodox Achaeans who worshipped Zagreus; but as we find no mention in Homer of oracular prophecies at Delphi, it may well be that the sanctuaries had not yet been re-established after the still-recent victory of the Epigoni. These sanctuaries, in particular that of Apollo, do not appear to have been looted during the Theban war, since they were still regarded as very wealthy.[295]

Finally, one of the most interesting details in the Catalogue of Ships, from our point of view, is the presence of an Arcadian contingent, to whom Agamemnon gave sixty vessels, since these inland people had no coastline, and 'hitherto had never concerned themselves with marine matters'.[296] Of the nine regions named, those we can identify are situated either on the high upland plateau of Tripolis, or down in the valleys, where cattle-grazing was possible—though Orchomenus in Arcadia is described as being 'rich in sheep'. Here too, after the fall of Thebes, the accessible regions had asked nothing better than to rally to the right side, repudiating Dionysus and his orgies.

We should not forget that for Homer man is still a wholly rational being. Dionysus is banned from decent society. Passions such as anger, love, or religious ecstasy are afflictions sent by the gods. It was quite inconceivable, therefore, that any man should not act in his own best interests. If he failed to do so, this was merely proof that some supra-human power had worked against him and stopped him being his true self. Such a concept must assume imperfection in the gods, since if they *were* perfect, why should they prevent a man acting in his own best interests? But this objection takes the problem of evil into account, and the ideal which Homer lays before mankind is, essentially, heroic: it is his complete self-fulfilment on the plane of rational, predictable conduct. This ideal is not as yet humanistic—that is, a harmonious balance of all human faculties in discreet moderation [*sōphrosyné*]; there is a great gulf between Homer and Pythagoras, between the hero and the man of measure.[297] In any case, these Dionysiac transports could not be admitted into the Achaean world without destroying it. This, indeed, was how it perished: its concept of man could not survive the wine and goatishness and Maenadic frenzies. Aphrodite, too, was ranged against it; she was the mother of Harmonia, Cadmus's wife. The slow emergence of the irrational, the crystallisation of certain beliefs in a tangible form, and their fatal incompatibility with other existing patterns especially the heroic-rational one—here we see one crucial factor in that bloody drama which finally destroyed the whole brilliant civilisation of Bronze Age Greece.

It is fashionable to interpret the war of the Seven, the expedition of the Epigoni, and the campaign against Troy in purely economic terms;[298] and no doubt they did all have some such underlying cause. But this type of motivation had long since bred others, at an emotional, non-rational level, where such impulses become a thousand times harder to control or eradicate. None of the wars in the Bronze Age were undertaken solely in the hope of acquiring booty; and indeed, as I have already emphasised, the Achaeans—in contrast to their contemporaries the Hittites—do not appear to have been a race of natural warriors. Furthermore, when we study Greece's unique geographical position, we may well conclude that it offered raiders little return for their trouble. The Achaeans seem never to have gone in for piracy, and the age of tribute-payment had not yet dawned. The group which conquered Crete in 1405 settled there to enjoy the fruits of their victory. Tlepolemus, fleeing from the Heraclidae, took refuge on Rhodes with his followers, and proceeded to establish an independent kingdom. But throughout their brilliant history, which lasted at least half a millennium (if we accept Palmer's 'short' chronology), or far longer, according to the traditional extended date-scheme, the Achaeans never once showed themselves actively adventurous. Colonisation had no attraction for them. To protect themselves against internal danger they had one idea, and one only: fortified enclosures. They do not appear to have been tempted to steal anything from their neighbours—a few pieces of bronze, perhaps, a little gold, a handful of slaves. Their real wealth lay in their herds of cattle, which could only with great difficulty be transported for long distances by sea; while their great storage-jars [*pithoi*] and the wheat or oil inside them were, to all intents and purposes, fixtures. There must have been far more compelling motives than the prospect of immediate gain (except perhaps in the case of the conquest of Crete) to force the Achaean world into concerted actions so memorable that their story was faithfully passed on from those dark years of prehistory until the present day. I have attempted to demonstrate that it was a combination of social and religious pressures that finally drove the rich landed proprietors of Achaea to undertake their campaigns against Thebes, which only ended with the city's destruction. Yet when they had smashed this hotbed of heresy and sedition, and equipped their country with a defence system that allowed them full liberty of movement, the first thing the Achaeans did, without any delay, was to turn against Troy. Why? We have already touched on their motives, but now our historical narrative has reached the year 1250, when the great Achaean fleet assembled at Aulis, it may be helpful to recapitulate them once more.

Archaeology has not confirmed Homer's descriptions of Troy. The splendid legend of Troy VI has ousted the miserable reality of Troy VIIa, the city the Achaeans actually destroyed between 1250 and 1240. The earthquake which devastated Troy VI was still too recent a memory to have been forgotten by the Greek chieftains who took part in this expedition, much less unknown to them—especially since Troy VIIa's trade with the west, though much reduced, had never ceased altogether. It is impossible for Agamemnon and his barons *not* to have known perfectly well that proud Ilium was, in their day, no more than a poverty-stricken town, run up by squatters among the devastated ruins of Troy VI; that even the local pottery was now no more than a bad imitation of those beautiful Mycenaean vases which in previous generations they had exported abroad. The Achaean empire was far too well organised—and, as the Pylos tablets prove, this minutely detailed administrative system lasted right to the very end—for its government to have made the error of supposing that they would be any the richer by acquiring Troy, which in their day was a derisory prize.

No; we have to look elsewhere for the causes of the Trojan War. Like the wars over Thebes, they were of a socio-religious nature. Moreover, the Achaeans were not so far out in their calculations: this preventive war won them a respite of more than a century. When we weigh up all the evidence, Agamemnon may well have been a better statesman than common opinion will allow.

I have already outlined the social conditions which, in their turn, gave rise to religious antagonism. Homer was still aware that ox-eyed Hera, Poseidon the tamer of horses, and Hephaestus the bronze-worker, all fought consistently on the side of the Achaeans, whereas the Trojans were always supported by the Dionysiac pantheon: Phoebus, his sister Artemis, and Aphrodite, whose connections with the Cadmeans were common knowledge.

Troy's impoverishment—the prime cause of emigration amongst her inhabitants—must have created a majority of goat-worshippers there in the period after 1300. This would go far to explain the atmosphere of hatred and fanaticism, not to mention the curious tradition according to which Troy was subjugated by Heracles, long before the Achaean expedition[299]—a piece of special pleading which, by attributing Ilium's entry into the Theban circle to *force majeure*, attempted to relieve its inhabitants of responsibility for so unreasonable a choice.

Thucydides, as we have seen, was no admirer of the Achaeans. It must be remembered that in his day the science of archaeology was non-existent, and that no one could have read the Linear B tablets even if their existence had been known—which it was not. His verdict (and he may not be so far out) is that the strategy of the period was crazy;[300] it seems likely that it had long since been an anachronism, and a century later its utter ineffectuality stood revealed for all to see. But the cavalry has throughout history invariably tended towards diehard conservatism. Agincourt and Chaeronea were both, strategically speaking, nonsensical; and one only has to read Sir Winston Churchill's account of the last cavalry charge with drawn sabres to see what lunacies an exaggerated love of panache can bring in its wake.

Thucydides seems no more impressed by the size of the Greek army. There was, he tells us, an overall complement of twelve hundred ships. The largest were those contributed by the Boeotians, each of which carried a hundred and twenty men, all combatants; the smallest were those of Philoctetes, which accommodated fifty. Taking the mean average, we obtain a figure of eighty-five men per vessel, which would work out at a grand total of 100,000 fighting men. Thucydides does not regard this army as particularly large for an expedition sponsored by all the Greek states in common.[301] We, being more distant from the event, may nevertheless feel that 100,000 men is an impressive enough figure; but Thucydides was probably not allowing for the division of the Achaean empire—a factor which would, inevitably, produce some complex problems of supply and revictualling, as Thucydides himself, with his habitual insight, indicates elsewhere. But we may well concede a point to the historian of the Peloponnesian War when he says that under better leadership this force could have seized Troy VIIa without the slightest difficulty: the city's paltry 450 yards of ramparts cannot have constituted a very formidable obstacle.

Be that as it may, and despite the immense drain a ten years' campaign must have made upon the resources of a limited group of citizens, the Trojan War seems to have ended to the advantage of the Achaeans. As we have seen, the Trojans were, beyond a doubt, annihilated, and their power destroyed for ever. The Achaean princes returned home in pomp and fine array to enjoy the fruits of their victory: only Agamemnon seems to have met a dramatic end in no way connected with those historical forces I am attempting to isolate here, but due to the infidelity of a wife who loved her paramour all too well.

After Orestes had re-established his family's claim to the throne of Mycenae, about 1225, the Achaean empire returned to its customary occupations, that is, the breeding of cattle and horses.[302] Nevertheless, agriculture had in the meanwhile made great advances: canal-ditching was begun about now at Orchomenus, with a view to draining part of the Copaic marsh and turning it into arable land—clearly at the expense of pasturage, which makes it a most interesting sign of the times.[303] There was also the trade in perfumed oil,[304] which must have been one of Achaea's most profitable exports: this passion for oiling oneself was constant throughout the Aegean world. Another source of wealth may well have been copper. An ancient copper-mine has been discovered near Nemea—and therefore within easy reach of Mycenae. Others may well have existed.[305]

The Linear B tablets show us what important items wheat and barley, together with oil and dried figs, had become in the Achaean people's diet. But all these commodities were sternly rationed, and the quantities allowed were insufficient to maintain a hard-working manual labourer. Furthermore, we possess evidence suggesting that far more meat was consumed during the Bronze Age than in the classical period.[306] This is only natural, but—as between equal areas—stock-farming can support far fewer people than agriculture.

The capture of Thebes and the destruction of Troy must, temporarily at least, have discouraged the immigration of nomadic herdsmen. But Bronze Age civilisation was caught in the vicious circle set up by its very success. Wars were never undertaken except by the nobles who owned the rich pastureland; and meanwhile the goatherds grew and multiplied. When peace returned, the problem of over-population became more acute than ever.

Orestes succeeded to the throne of his uncle, Menelaus:[307] and though he was undoubtedly a strong and capable monarch, it is safe to assume that by his day the *status quo* had become so traditional that the problems seemed to admit of no solution: the new King of Mycenae could only do what his predecessors had done, which was to build and contract for more walls, fresh Cyclopean strongholds to defend himself against his internal enemies.

At Mycenae itself he added the third ring-wall to the fortress enclosure. The curious form and narrow entrance-gate of this ring-wall leads one to suppose that it was intended to protect the royal horses against raids by the mountain herdsmen, who were now intensifying their activities. It was now that the extraordinary underground passage to the cistern-well was constructed: after more than thirty centuries its cement remains as waterproof as ever. Mycenae was now in a position to withstand a lengthy siege. Orestes' provisions must have been based on a gloomy assessment of the future—and with good reason. Perhaps he could no longer even count on the loyalty of many of his supporters. Tiryns and Argos still provided the stockades for Mycenae's cattle. (See Plate 21.)

At about the same time the Pelargicum was built in Athens. This seems to have comprised (1) a small triangular extension at the northwest corner of the Acropolis, well below the level of the primitive fortress, and only accessible by ladders; and (2) a cattle stockade, on the present site of the Herodes Atticus theatre, which probably utilised the south gate, this being in an open position between the fortress enclosure and the Tower of Victory.[308]

It is certain that many other defensive constructions (at Asine especially, and Dyme in Achaea) date back to this period; but full confirmation must await further archaeological work *in situ*. We may note that the third enclosure at Mycenae and the Pelargicum in Athens both contained wells or springs, and the system whereby Tiryns' cattle stockade was supplied with water has also recently come to light. The situation which the Linear B tablets reveal to us is certainly a critical one. Goats, for all practical purposes, went untaxed since it was impossible to collect such a levy. The tax on sheep produced no more than a 50 per cent return. The small graziers were virtually immune to any attempts at coercion from the palace. Heavy livestock was seldom taxed: this exemption must have been a perquisite of the nobility. Often there was no more than one horse to a chariot.[309]

But Orestes must have been a remarkable man, with a firm grip on his kingdom. So long as he lived, and despite ever-increasing internal

19a A view of Dyme from the South-West

b Dyme: the gateway which was walled up in Byzantine times

20 A view of Dyme from the North-East

pressure, he managed to maintain the structure of the Greek world more or less as Agamemnon had left it. But about 1180 he died, and the removal of that iron hand allowed the first cracks to appear in the edifice of the Achaean empire. He left the crown to his son Tisamenus, but the succession was not accomplished without serious disturbances. A major revolt broke out in Messenia, and the palace of Pylos, which Neleus and Nestor had built, was burnt to the ground. It would have been interesting if the tablets baked in this fire had given us any indication as to whether the attack came from the seaward side; but in fact the tablets do not, however obliquely, suggest anything of the sort.[310] Besides, the destruction of Pylos was not accompanied by any signs of invasion, and the site was not reoccupied. Pylos only put up a slight resistance, and in any case its defences were in a bad state of repair. The passing of the great King must alone have sufficed to create a wave of mob-violence which swept away this heritage of the glorious past. The goatherds moved in at Ano Engliano: one can see them to this day, all round the excavations of the American School. They are very likeable people, and very proud of 'their' excavation. (See Plate 17.)

The new King of Mycenae, Tisamenus, would in all likelihood have been only too glad to come to his fellow sovereign's aid at Pylos; but, shut in behind the gigantic ramparts which his ancestors had built, he was hard put to it to defend himself, and whatever happened he could not conceivably have marched on Pylos. The tide of rebellion was lapping at the very walls of his citadel, and all the buildings outside the Cyclopean fortifications were burnt—including the precious perfumed-oil refinery, from which the king probably derived a good proportion of his revenues.[311]

It must have been now that a group of distinguished citizens from Pylos managed to escape, and sought asylum—which was granted—in Athens.[312] Among them were the ancestors both of Codrus and of Pisistratus.[313] These Pylians must have been men of some substance to have made such a mark in Attica; and Thucydides[314] is clearly justified when he says that Attica was always the refuge of the most capable [*dynatōtatoi*] people from every other part of Greece.[315]

However far back we go, we find that the peculiar aridity of Attica effectively precluded all internal rivalries and dissensions: her inhabitants always remained the same.[316] At the close of the Bronze Age she must have been spared that sharp division between rich and poor, between bullworshippers and goat-worshippers, which was soon to culminate in the final, tragic destruction of the Achaean world. The population of Attica, welded into a unity by the harsh land they inhabited,[317] could always take refuge on the rock-solid Athenian Acropolis,[318] now enlarged, modernised, and provided with water-points. Short of treachery amongst the ranks of the defenders, it was virtually impossible at this period to take such a fortress by storm or siege. It had taken the united forces of Achaea two bloody campaigns to reduce Thebes alone; and their great army, a hundred thousand strong, had spent ten long years besieging the miserable city that was Troy VIIa.

As subsequent events confirm, the Pylians who chose Athens as an asylum had gauged the morale of the Mycenaean fortresses' defenders all too accurately. The Achaean empire had revealed just how vulnerable it was. But it was still extremely wealthy, a magnificent potential prize that was bound to attract covetous glances. There were, first, the Heraclidae, who must still have been settled in the neighbourhood of Thebes, and who probably had not forgotten their humiliating defeat at the Isthmus wall in 1250. They, beyond a doubt, still coveted the Argive plain, which they regarded as theirs by right of ancestral possession. They found some unexpected allies in an obscure Greek tribe which had played scarcely any part in the brilliant evolution of the Bronze Age, their history being one of remote, inglorious isolation: the Dorians. Such an alliance is vouched for by Tyrtaeus,[319] and constitutes the first known historical reference to the Dorians. This small and remote tribe seems to have been universally unpopular, and was always being moved on from the various habitats in which it settled. Under Deucalion's rule the Dorians occupied Phthiotis in south-east Thessaly; during the reign of Dorus, Deucalion's son, they migrated to Histaeotis at the foot of the Pindus. When the Cadmeans left Thebes after the war of the Epigoni, they drove the Dorians out of Histaeotis, and the latter retreated southwards, to the foothills of Parnassus. From there they moved down to Dryopis, which they renamed Doris.[320] In the period after the Trojan War, then, the territory occupied by these backward Greeks was very small indeed, and no one seems to have taken any particular notice of them. The Achaeans, during their period of ascendancy, would have found them far easier to annihilate than the Trojans. But no man can see into the future, and the potential threat which these rude tribesmen represented seems not to have occurred to anyone.

The Dorians are often connected with the introduction of iron weapons. It is true that their invasion took place at a time when the use of iron was becoming more widespread, but the association of these backward people with the new technique has still to be proved archaeologically. In any case the name 'Dorian' means 'spearman' or 'fighter-with-a-spear',[321] which is not an especially appropriate epithet for a warrior whose weapons are of iron. Even when combined with the Heraclidae, these Dorians were surely not very numerous,[322] and in order to conquer the various Achaean strongholds they must have found powerful support among the local population, and maintained secret communications with traitors inside the fortresses themselves.

Their first operation proved abortive. Together with the Heraclidae they invaded Attica shortly before 1160. But the bloody revolution they had anticipated failed to materialise.[323] From this we may conclude that the section of the population which had everything to gain by a sudden and violent change of régime was too small to make itself felt. It appears that the Dorians twice attempted to storm the Acropolis,[324] but failed to dislodge the inhabitants, who could continue to boast that they—as personified by their ancestor Erechtheus[325]—were born of the very soil of Attica, where none had preceded them. The fortress which secured them their victory became a sacred monument: temples were built there, and even the cattle stockade of the Pelargicum was regarded as holy ground, where no man might dwell.[326]

The defeated tribesmen were forced to withdraw into Doris again: it was probably now that they overran the strongholds of Boeotia. They must have found all the reinforcements they could hope for in the mountain country round Lake Copaïs, and in all likelihood various spies and traitors inside the fortresses themselves, since to mount an assault on the great ramparts of Gla would, in those days, have been a formidable undertaking. But these newcomers did not settle down in lush Boeotia: the Heraclidae had their eye on Tiryns, while the Dorians coveted Mycenae and its gold.

It seems very likely that from Boeotia the Dorians made their way back through Doris once more, since the passes on this side are easy of access. From Erineus they descended on Naupactus,[327] where they built themselves a fleet of rafts and made the short crossing into the Peloponnese, thus outflanking the Isthmus wall. Without pressing the parallel too far, we may say that these new invaders fulfilled the same role as the Cadmeans had done two centuries earlier: they provided a rallying-point for malcontents. All the mountain herdsmen must have hastened to join them, eager for a chance, at last, to burn and sack the fortresses of their detested overlords. But the Cadmeans had been highly civilised people, who used this rebellious rabble to consolidate their own power in Thebes, where they not only led a most elegant and cultured existence, but also undertook so magnificent a building programme that its fame continued to echo down the centuries after they were gone. In the presesent case, however, nothing of the sort occurred. Once all the cattle had been slaughtered and eaten, no one was interested in renovating the burnt fortress. The Dorians settled in a series of squalid little villages, whole centuries of civilisation were lost as though they had never been, and man had once more to climb painfully up the slope which leads from a wattled hut to the palace of Mycenae. But the Heraclidae were avenged; the Goat, at long last, had triumphed over the Bull. The process is an illogical one, but then man is illogical too; and if we fail to make due allowance for his emotional and religious prejudices, how can we hope to understand why he should destroy a well-nigh indestructible palace and then camp out in the rain? Exactly the same phenomenon can be observed, centuries later, after the fall of the Roman Empire.

Pausanias tells us that this 'return of the Heraclidae' devastated the entire Peloponnese with the exception of Arcadia,[328] and adds that before the coming of the Heraclidae both Athens and Argos spoke the same language.[329] This is not, *au fond*, impossible: Ionian might well have developed, during the Dark Ages, from Arcado-Cypriot, which must have been the dialect most akin to that spoken by Achaeans in the days of the empire, and now read by us on the Linear B tablets.

It seems a foregone conclusion that the Dorians must have had secret supporters inside the strongholds they besieged. Without this they could never have taken them: they were impregnable. Nor should we forget that the Achaean nobility fought according to a strict code, and, in true chivalrous fashion, perhaps preferred death with honour to the idea of lowering themselves to the level of this vulgar rabble, which knew nothing about the art of war or epic minstrelsy. History contains instances of collective suicide (the Etruscans bear witness to this), and to die for one's God is sometimes considered a privilege.

So the Dorians gradually extended their sway over the south and east of the Peloponnese, where their arrival, as Wace remarks,[330] is far more suggestive of a new political régime than of an invasion. Those of them who had stayed behind in Doris, at the foot of Parnassus, finally migrated again, to the distant Adriatic coast, travelling as far north as Corcyra before they finally settled. This corresponds to the distribution of the Dorian dialect in historical times, though we should not draw any over-dogmatic conclusions from the fact: in four or five

21 Orestes's door at Mycenae

22a Examples of L.H. IIIc ware

b A close style pot

centuries people are liable to change their habitat, and we know, in particular, what a prodigious effort it cost the Dorians to impose their authority on Messenia. Above all, our documentation for this period is very sparse indeed. Let us therefore treat it with discretion.

The Dorians preserved the existing division in the population: they had 'Helots', who were slaves in the new, full sense of the word, and 'Perioeci', or 'dwellers-round-about', second-class citizens established in the foothills. It needs little effort to deduce that the Helots were their enemies, the former Achaean cattle-graziers; while the Perioeci were the mountain goatherds who had supported and aided them during the invasion, and now, as a reward, were permitted to keep the harsh, barren uplands they had previously occupied.

Then comes a rather lengthy pause that must have corresponded to local revolutions and counter-revolutions. One of these counter-revolutions seems to have met with some success at Mycenae and during some twenty years a royal house was responsible for the production of the 'closed style' pottery.[331] But in the end the revolution was victorious all over the country and the Achaeans lost the Peloponnese before 1100.

After this interval of about half a century, the Dorians and their followers made one final sortie. They invaded Crete. Here, too, the Achaeans seem not to have offered any sort of organised resistance. The attackers burnt everything and rebuilt nothing. In Crete, again, the Dorians preserved the division of the population into two classes: the *aphamiotai* or *klarotai*, who were slaves in the classical sense of the word, and the *mnoitai*, who were peasants working the village land in return for a small pittance.[332] Again, it is not hard to work out that the *aphamiotai* were the descendants of the Dorians' enemies, the one-time big stock-farmers, while the *mnoitai* were the goatherds who had helped the invaders.[333]

The splendid adventure of the Bronze Age was over. Those who had lived through it perished, as Hesiod says, by their own hand, and went to dwell in dank Hades, leaving no name behind them.[334] Yet this squalid end is part of a classic pattern. In a disorganised society which has lost all faith in itself anything can happen.[335] The Vandals—and they numbered no more than 80,000, women and children included—were to re-enact the Dorian adventure in a Roman setting. Yet Thucydides regarded the Achaeans' feat in assembling 100,000 combatants before the walls of Troy as a negligible effort! One is tempted to ask what the Vandals might not have achieved with a similar force at their disposal.

CHAPTER V

The Aftermath

As we have seen, Attica undoubtedly served as a place of refuge for those Achaeans who contrived to escape[336] both the Dorians and the Heraclidae coming down from the north, and the goatherds descending from their mountain fastnesses. It looks, indeed, as though Athens received such an influx of refugees that the cemeteries were too small to cope with them: this is one explanation for the sudden reappearance, shortly after 1100, of cremation—a practice which was to last for a century and more.[337]

Yet the lesson of the catastrophe, which had been directly brought about by overpopulation during the latter part of the Bronze Age, was not lost on subsequent generations. Well before the year 1000, emigration to the other side of the Aegean was already a well-established trend in Attica.[338] Tradition even has it that certain cities of Aeolia, Cyme in particular, were founded earlier still, by groups of emigrants.[339]

The fusion of these refugees with the local population, who were certainly Ionian by origin,[340] produced an exceptionally gifted race. Dynamic, imaginative, individualistic, they were largely responsible for what we know as the 'Greek miracle'. It may be of interest to note that, in ceramics and poetry alike, the Achaean contribution to Ionian culture is enormous, and in fact forms a departure-point for this new period of creativity.

As far as Attic ware is concerned, the first attempts at representational art (whether of humans or animals) do not seem to go back beyond the beginning of the eighth century B.C.; and even then these early friezes show us processions of Achaean chariots, and warriors with huge Mycenaean figure-of-eight shields made of oxhide—shields that by now could be nothing but dim memories in legend or, at best, archaic curiosities, though one or two examples may have survived, probably as ex-voto offerings hung up in temples. The chariots, too, were almost certainly drawn without an actual model, from descriptions given in epic poetry. By and large they are quite impossible, and can never have existed as portrayed here. Sometimes, too, the artist, in an absent-minded moment, turns one of these obsolete war-chariots into a common four-wheeled cart such as existed in his own day.

It must have been at more or less the same period that Homer, using the new alphabetic script, set down and 'fixed' the famous exploits of these Achaean heroes in Ionian hexameters. Centuries of oral tradition[341] had preserved the myths concerning them, and turned them into legendary figures; but it is also clear, beyond any reasonable doubt, that this long oral tradition had preserved numerous characteristically Mycenean elements[342] which only the Achaean refugees in Attica could have known and passed on.

But the rhythm of this epic poetry came, in the end, to influence all Ionian art,[343] so that its geometric friezes, for instance, differed radically from the designs favoured by a city such as Corinth, which had been led down different aesthetic paths as a result of her Oriental contacts. Above all, the Achaeans' ethical concept of man as a wholly rational creature, their notion of the imperfect god who fights *with* his worshipper, but *for whom* his worshipper never fights,[344] must have remained a powerful latent influence on the Athenian subconscious mind at least till Plato's era—and indeed much later, as the example of Constantine the Great shows us: Platonism only became a real influence when it assumed neo-Platonic dress.

The ancient Helladic distinction—it goes back at least to the Bronze Age—between those who use horses and those who go on foot was not to be obliterated for centuries. Throughout all Greek history the infantry remained an essentially Dorian institution, while the first treatise on the equestrian art was written by Xenophon the Athenian, a distant descendant of the men who had driven their chariots across the Argive plain. All this was still bound up with the survival of the bitter hatred between followers of the Bull and followers of the Goat—a hatred that rankled on for generations, long after its emblems had lost all social and symbolic significance, in a world whose fertility myths were no longer animal but vegetable: man lived primarily by agriculture now, and stock-farming had become of secondary importance.

This tenacious hatred is reflected very clearly in the serious and deliberate efforts we find being made, not once but many times, at Delphi or Eleusis or Olympia, to fuse these two ancestral religions in a common faith that would have united Greece. But it is not so easy to mould man's unconscious mind.

Yet as early as Homer we come across a new intoxicating and prophetic beverage which seeks to replace wine and hydromel alike, uniting their adherents in a single, identical inebriety. This is the *kykéon*, a mixture of wine, honey, goat's cheese and barley-gruel.[345] At first sight the recipe is not, clearly, one with universal appeal: and yet it was with the aid of a similar cocktail that Circe managed to seduce Odysseus.[346] This attempt at alcoholic syncretism must have had a long and curious history,[347] for when agriculture replaced stock-breeding in Greece the new fertility-myth was naturally associated with Demeter, who had become goddess of the harvest, and with her daughter Koré. Their principal sanctuary was at Eleusis; and it was the ancient, venerable and syncretic *kykéon* that became the ritual drink consumed there during the celebration of the Mysteries, themselves bound up with the annual and miraculous rebirth of the vegetable world.[348] If we examine the *Homeric Hymn to Demeter*, moreover, we may well conclude that this liquor, for all its magical properties, did not invariably contain wine. Perhaps, on especially solemn ritual occasions, men still partook of that primitive liquor, the produce of the sacred Delphic hive, whose formula certainly went back to before 1400 B.C. Myths often survive for the most extraordinary length of time. In the Orphic version of this vegetation-myth, the magical powers of the rite are, naturally, extended till they embrace the whole natural world. Now Demeter is welcomed at Eleusis by a shepherd (Eumolpus), an oxherd (Triptolemus), a goatherd (Dysaulus), and a swineherd (Eubulus)—not to mention a prostitute. By now Demeter is responsible not only for good harvests but also for the fertility of sheep, bulls, goats, pigs, and human beings. The author's only omission, it would seem, is the horse. This apart, one could hardly go further in an effort to syncretise the conflicting traditions and leanings inherited from the Mycenaean age.

I have had occasion to speak of the late myths which crystallised about the person of Aristaeus, and of their persistent survival until, by the first century A.D., they had become the merest absurdities. In the end Aristaeus was credited not only with the introduction of bee-keeping and viticulture, but also with teaching men the art of stockbreeding —cattle, sheep and goats alike. In other words, this new myth set out to show that Aristaeus successfully reconciled, in his own person, the origins of the two rival fertility-myths, which henceforth would be blended in a single form.[349]

The syncretism practised at Delphi was on a far more profound level. There was now one fertility-god only, with characteristics of both Bull and Goat—Dionysus. But his former adherent, Apollo (originally the god of sailors, who steered their course by the sun, but now promoted into a full-blown solar deity, and thus identified with reason and light), was still left standing, a golden image, above the tomb whence the irrational principle—fertile, sexually potent—would be endlessly renewed under his divine dispensation.[350] The symbolism which this admirable syncretic myth incorporates stems from ideas of harmonious balance, humane tolerance, *sóphrosýne* (discreet moderation): we have come a long way from the heroic age of Mycenae.

There had been numerous other attempts to avoid the final catastrophe of a direct, head-on clash: these reveal a far more traditional and Homeric way of thinking, but some of them, nevertheless, display the most subtle ingenuity. We find Zeus born in Crete as a Bull-god, but reared by a she-goat. Zagreus becomes his son by Persephone, just as Dionysus was by Semele. When the Titans had committed their act of *sparagmós*—that is, when they had torn Zagreus into seven ritual pieces—Zeus struck them down with his thunderbolt. Then he interred the seven fragments of his son in a tomb that was both *omphalos* and sacred hive. From here the divine martyr was reborn—but in Dionysiac form, so that Dionysus found himself associated with the Bull despite his goatish entourage.

It is thus that we find him in the literature of the classical period, especially in the syncretic myth which Euripides developed when composing the *Bacchae*. This myth presents a Dionysus born of Zeus and Semele but still retaining his associations with the Bull. The result is a complex deity, whose double origin (the two halves of which are, perhaps, in the last resort irreconcilable) endows him with the violent temperament produced by instinctive, uncontrolled passion, *and* with that lofty indifference bred of absolute authority. It is not easy to be, at one and the same time, both bounding Goat and dominating Bull. For all his genius, I think we are justified in asking whether Euripides really succeeded in giving his central character divine stature.

After the fall of Athens, the Hellenistic era's insipid climate of thought soon reduced Dionysus's stature: from the god of the irrational *force vitale* he was rapidly transmogrified into the god of tippling and casual amours. Zeus conceived a passion for his cup-bearer. Finally the Christians relegated the Goat to Hell (having invented the idea of sin as counterpart to a perfect god) while the Bull ascended to Heaven and became the emblem of St Luke.

Are the two principles really irreconcilable? Certainly they seem to have been so in Greece. Despite the efforts to reconcile them (which were carried out, to some extent, at every level) the hatred existing between the Bull's and the Goat's supporters remained perennial and inextinguishable, a legacy to their descendants. It led to the Peloponnesian War, in which, once again, the central essence of the Greek spirit was destroyed. But the Greeks of the classical period were more fortunate than their Bronze Age predecessors in one sense: at least they found, in the Romans, a people prepared to keep their heritage alive, to accept it and adapt it naturally for their own uses. This process did not distort the tradition to the point where it became unrecognisable; the legacy of the second Greek miracle[351] was never really lost.

Such obscure but obstinate attachments to two separate fertility-myths do not, of course, constitute the only detectable explanation of those internecine conflicts which, from the Bronze Age onwards, divided Greek from Greek. But if we do not make due allowance for them—and they form a basic element in all religions, they go back to the heroic age, to that period of prehistory when the Greeks still lived almost exclusively by stock-farming—then the savage fanaticism of those struggles we witness in the historical era, when men lived primarily by trade, industry and agriculture, when they strove to exercise their reason, to reconcile Apollo with Dionysus, must strike us as wholly inexplicable.

Bibliographical Note

THE bibliography of Greek and Cretan Bronze Age history is a vast one, and easy enough to compile. Specialists are well acquainted with it already, and in their case such a supplementary list would serve no useful purpose, but be a mere gratuitous display of erudition. For the lay reader, however, the question is considerably more delicate. He should, if he is to avoid being led into error, exercise a high degree of selectivity in his choice of reading matter. Let me try to explain why.

In the field of Greek Bronze Age studies, the three basic groups of scholarly works are those, respectively, of Schliemann, Evans, and Ventris: each has his followers or 'school'. No one, as far as I know, any longer makes serious use of texts by the Schliemann group, which are now no more than archaeological curiosities. On the other hand, the works of Evans and his adherents are still widely read and used—wrongly, in my opinion. The chronological scheme which Evans proposed is no more acceptable than his historical theories, while the countless confusions and omissions with which his reports abound render his monumental labours invalid. To quote Doro Levi, perhaps the scholar best qualified to pronounce on this matter, we must wipe the board clean and start afresh (see *Parola del Passato*, vol. 71 (1960), p. 120.) Only the specialist is used to sorting the wheat from the chaff; the layman is doomed to instant defeat.

It should be held in mind that anyhow for the Greek Bronze Age period, there is a triple chain of evidence all three strands of which must agree with one another constantly: if they do not, it means that the interpretation placed on some fact is false and must be revised. The triple chain consists of (*a*) history, (*b*) archaeology, and (*c*) linguistics. I have listed these disciplines at random, and in point of fact they possess an equal importance. When a hypothesis satisfies all three, one can confidently declare it to be the truth, since the chance of two different possibilities existing that would satisfy the innumerable requirements of all three disciplines is so small, for all practical purposes, as to be negligible.

Naturally, in this kind of field one can never *prove* anything. Proofs fall into the category of logic and mathematics, and I have dealt with them elsewhere *in extenso* (*Apollon et Dionysos*, Les Belles Lettres, Paris 1961). Here we have to balance *probabilities;* and the pedantic trick of saying, with a superior air, 'Prove it' is a facile gambit, and no adequate substitute for judgment or knowledge.

If, however, in the three branches of knowledge I have mentioned, we reject the works of Schliemann, Evans and all their followers (today this is the only possible course for the lay reader to follow), then the ground is quickly cleared, and the choice of reading-matter much reduced.

(*a*) *History*

The basic work is that by Professor L. R. Palmer, *Mycenaeans and Minoans* (London 1961)* together with the review-essay by G. Mylonas, in *Hesperia*, Vol. 31/3 (1962), attempting to refute it. Naturally ancient literature, called usually classical, which now comprises the B tablets, is our real source in every sense of the word.

(*b*) *Archaeology*

Here the field is much wider. For the chronology of Mycenaean pottery, A. Furumark's *Mycenaean Pottery: Analysis and Classification* and *The Chronology of Mycenaean Pottery* (Stockholm 1941) are still valuable. They also contain date-schemes for Cypriot and Philistine pottery.

From the geographical standpoint, Cyprus lies rather outside the field covered in this book but its story can be related in a perfect way to our tale. For Cyprus there exists a remarkable archaeological book: H. W. Catling's *Cypriot Bronze Work in the Mycenaean World* (Oxford 1964). The scope of this work is broader than its title suggests. Here, in brief, are the facts which relate Cyprus to our tale:

Very few Egyptian finds have been made in Cyprus and one single Hittite object came to light. (Cyprus must certainly not be identified with Alasia.)

Three totally different phases must be distinguished in the relations of Cyprus with the Aegean.

(1) Up to the end of the period L.H.IIIa (see Furumark's table) exchanges are most active, exchanges firmly based on local copper; but

* Unfortunately I have been unable to use the revised edition (1965) of this work as it did not appear in time.

during this period there existed no permanent Mycenaean establishment in Cyprus.

(2) Then in the thirteenth century relations become much less frequent. As we know, the Achaeans were busy fighting their two wars against Thebes, and then sailed for Troy.

(3) In the period L.H.IIIc, that is after 1240, a very important group of Achaeans settled in Cyprus. The remains of their buildings are as impressive as the remains of their tombs.

Here again the myths preserved recover a historical sequence that is easy to reconstruct, and which agrees perfectly with the archaeological interpretation. It is the myth of Teucer whose genealogical tree we give below. The Achaean establishment in Cyprus of L.H.IIIc corresponds to the migration *after* the Trojan war of Teucer from Salamis to Cyprus.[352]

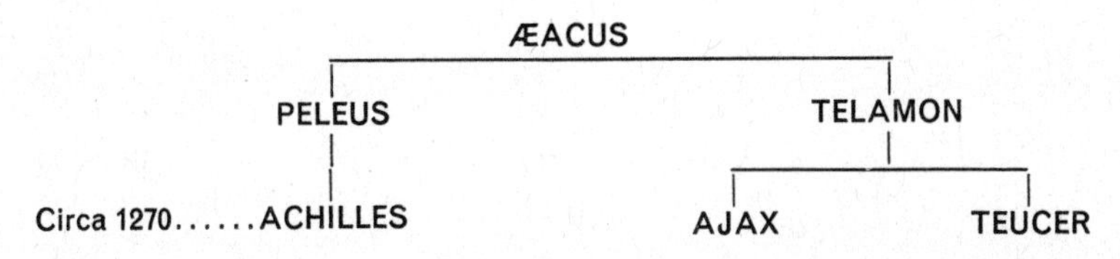

Teucer was the bastard [353] or more probably the legitimate[354] son of Telamon and brother of Ajax. For the alleged circumstances of his departure from his fatherland of Salamis and the foundation of the Cypriot Salamis[355] see (*inter alios*) the late tradition preserved by Horace.[356]

For Mycenae we have various articles by A. J. B. Wace, and his admirable book *Mycenae*: an Archaeological History and Guide (Princeton 1949)—though the chronology of the latter is somewhat out of date—together with Mylonas's study *Ancient Mycenae* (London 1957), which contains some excellent illustrations. As we have observed (see n. 18), the second part of Mylonas's date-scheme is at least half a century too late, and that of Blegen should be adopted instead.

For Troy we have the admirable reports by Blegen: as far as the topics treated in this book are concerned, it will suffice to consult his revised fascicle, 'Troy', in the *Cambridge Ancient History* (1961). For Pylos, again, we have the same scholar's impeccable articles and reports: see *A Companion to Homer*, ed. A. J. B. Wace and F. H. Stubbings (London 1962), pp. 362ff. [Troy] and 422ff. [Pylos]. For Athens there is the exhaustive study by S. Iakovides, *L'Acropole mycénienne d'Athènes*

(Athens 1962), with a most important introduction by Prof. Spyridon Marinatos. The existing literature on Tiryns needs revising and bringing up to date. For Gla, there are two articles in the *Bulletin de la Société Hellénique d'Archéologie* which are very much to the point. For Thebes the works by Keramopoulos are now out of date, and as far as I know no adequate literature exists: one has to go to the site. Excavations, as I have mentioned several times, are in progress, but their publication will take a long time.

The same applies to Orchomenus, the museum of which is situated at Chaeronea.

For Crete the layman is in a difficult position. Apart from the publications of the Italian School (almost all dealing with Phaestos) almost everything needs reinterpreting in the light of recent chronological theory. This is why I have included my own date-scheme for Cretan pottery in the present volume. No doubt it will be corrected and modified at various points, but in broad outline I am convinced of its accuracy. Emily Vermeule's *Greece in the Bronze Age* (The University of Chicago Press 1964) contains a great wealth of information, but the historical statements made in this book need careful sifting.

Over and above the various works cited here there are, of course, innumerable monographs published both by the Greek Archaeological Service and by the various foreign Schools of Archaeology working in Greece. These monographs contain all the basic and essential findings of archaeological research, but are somewhat inaccessible to the non-specialist and are not available in translation. I shall not mention any of these for fear I may omit others; but it is to their authors that I owe my biggest debt of gratitude.

(*c*) *Linguistic Studies*

Here the layman need consult three works only: *Documents in Mycenaean Greek*, by Michael Ventris and John Chadwick (Cambridge 1956); Chadwick's *The Decipherment of Linear B* (Cambridge 1958). It must, however, be admitted that Wace's optimism, when he wrote the preface to the first of these two volumes, has not so far been justified by later developments.

The third work of capital importance in this field is L. R. Palmer, *The Interpretation of Mycenaean Greek Texts* (The Clarendon Press, Oxford 1963).

I have published in the Swiss periodical *Dialectica* (Vol. 17, No. 68, December 15, 1963) a detailed article on the analogies that allowed Ventris's stupendous effort to succeed. I here tried to show that the greatest obstacle which Ventris had to overcome was the pan-Minoan dragon invented by Evans.

I regret having to produce a species of bibliography-by-omission. But the specialist can create his own list without any help from me; and as for the layman, the monumental errors committed in the past make it far more urgent for me to draw up a list of the works he should *not* read rather than those he should, if he is to form an even approximately accurate picture of this all-too-remote period.

Appendix 1

I WOULD like, here, to thank Prof. G. Mylonas for all the care with which he has read the French edition of this book and for the long note he took the trouble to write for me in his admirable Greek script.

Professor Mylonas will see that I have taken into account some of his suggestions and criticisms, but not all of them. And this is unavoidable because our outlooks cannot be exactly the same: Professor Mylonas is an archaeologist, I am a humanist and a historian.

As I have already pointed out in the bibliography of this book, for the Bronze Age in Greece there exists a triple series of sources, all of the same importance, and these three categories must always be made to coincide in every proposed explanation. They are:

(1) History, which deals with the written and epigraphical tradition including now the B tablets.

(2) Linguistics, which studies the languages and dialects of the epoch under consideration.

(3) Archaeology, which studies the material remains left by the above-mentioned civilisation.

We must never forget that man has no direct access to any physical fact, be it archaeological, historical, linguistic or other. We always use certain interpretations of certain perceptions (some might say sense-data) reached through concepts that are usually highly abstract and very complicated. This problem of the nature of knowledge is crucial but far from simple. I have discussed it *in extenso*, including its mathematical and symbolical-logical aspects, in my book *Apollo and Dionysos* (Les Belles Lettres, Paris 1961) and I cannot detail these difficult arguments here.

All that we need for the present is to bear in mind that these concepts, which we use in order to interpret a given set of perceptions, follow the evolution of man in time. And so truth (always a provisional definition) changes with the form of the concepts that are in use: the earth has been really flat, really spherical, really ellipsoidal, etc. It seems to make a lot of truths. And the situation is exactly the same in the fields of history, of archaeology, of linguistics.

The other epistemological consequence that we must respect is that it can be shown that the definition 'truth' is unique at every given epoch. This means that there exists only one single definition compatible with all the concepts accepted at this given epoch. Therefore, in the frame of this provisional 'truth' (absolute truth is inaccessible to man), the historical evidence has exactly the same value as the linguistic one, or the archaeological one.

That a certain place should have been known by a certain name, or that it should have been associated with certain traditions, is part of the admitted 'truth' exactly in the same way as the fact that a certain sort of pottery has, or has not, been found in this place. After all, we want to write the story of the potters, not the story of the pots. But the human element that must, by necessity, be here associated with the purely archaeological knowledge—this human element is of infinite complexity and totally irrational. If one does not here (and for the Bronze Age in Greece it is always possible) turn for help to the written tradition and to the linguistic analysis of this tradition, there does not, in the general case, exist one single path leading from the pot to the potter: usually an infinity of conclusions are possible. Here lies the immense difficulty of writing about prehistoric times.

Bearing in mind this irrational nature of the human element, it seems to me always preferable to take the written tradition (by nature irrational) as starting-point for any historical reconstruction and to seek from this vantage-point the aid of archaeology and linguistics, with all the analogies and precisions that they can bring, especially when the written tradition is of a mythical nature.

Archaeology, the most exacting and fascinating science, is certainly a full-time job, and the same can be said of linguistics, the very difficult study and comparison of ancient languages. The study of the written tradition, let us call it humanism for short, is also a life-long job.

If there existed a genius capable of mastering all three of these disciplines, then this man would certainly be the only person entitled to write history. But such a genius has never existed in the past and the constant broadening of the fields of investigation makes it less and less likely every day that he will appear in the future. So we must resign ourselves to specialisation and the humanist must borrow from the archaeologist and from the linguist the technical knowledge that he himself cannot acquire, but that remains nevertheless indispensable for his interpretation of the human tradition. (See Appendix 2.)

As I have already pointed out, I think that we must always (whenever possible) start from the human tradition because of its irrational character. To go the other way round is an exercise fraught with dangers, and all modern theories thus built have turned out to be disastrous, from the Phoenician occupation of Mycenae to the grandiose pan-Minoan theories, and so many others.

This book is, as far as I know, the first attempt to write a coherent history of the Greek Bronze Age. Such an attempt can naturally not be final. No doubt many points of my tale may be corrected. There is also a great amount of digging still to be done. Furthermore, I believe that a deeper study of the written tradition might yield new results—in particular, I hope, the sequence of the Athenian dynasty that I was unable to unscramble from the myths. Pylos and Cyprus could be brought into the picture right now, their chronology presents no real difficulty,[357] and Rhodes would repay a special study, as I have already pointed out, because of the Hittite correspondence.

But, on the whole, I think that my tale makes sense, humanly, linguistically and archaeologically. I think that the motives invoked, the passions involved, are plausible. And because of this I think that on the whole the potters did what I describe for the reasons that I ascribe.

Appendix 2

THE ROLE OF ANALOGY IN THE DECIPHERMENT OF 'LINEAR B' MYCENAEAN WRITING

I. *The Problem*

The decipherment by Michael Ventris of the Mycenaean script known as 'Linear B' will always remain one of the greatest achievements in philology. This was the first system of writing to be elucidated without the aid of a bilingual text, by relying entirely on the use of *internal analogy* discernible in the various forms of the graphic structure. The special difficulties which Ventris had to overcome make his feat all the more remarkable.

The nineteenth century did not believe in the reality of the world as described by Homer and in particular in his 'Golden Mycenae'—until that day in 1876 when Schliemann revealed to their astounded gaze the famous tombs known today as the 'Mycenaean A circle', with their gold masks, jewels, encrusted weapons and ceramics.[1] At first, Schliemann believed he had discovered the tombs of Agamemnon and his companions; but he was later persuaded that these dated from a much earlier epoch than the Trojan war.[2] He finally agreed with his architect Dorpfeld[3] that they had uncovered the sepulchres of Phoenician settlers destroyed during the Dorian invasion,[4] a theory that was still being subscribed to in the 'thirties.

[1] Schliemann, being guided by Pausanias's text, excavated only the five tombs mentioned by that author. Tsoundas later discovered a sixth.

[2] The Trojan war took place in 1250 B.C., and the tombs of the 'A circle' date from about 1500 B.C. In Schliemann's time the Trojan war was thought to have taken place at a later date.

[3] Letter from Schliemann to Vichow, 18 June 1885.

[4] The Dorian invasion was quite unknown to ancient authors. The two verses of the Odyssey which mention the Dorians (*Od.* XIX. 177) are a later inter-

After having attempted in vain to purchase the site of the old palace of Cnossos in Crete from the Turks for excavation, Schliemann died in 1891. The political situation in 1899 enabled a rich young Englishman, Arthur Evans, the curator of the Ashmolean Museum in Oxford, to carry Schliemann's last wish into execution. He bought the Kephala site near Herakleion (Candia) and, under the auspices of the British School of Archeology, began excavating the famous hillock.

Only one product of the excavations is discussed here—the tablets which came to light almost immediately, all inscribed with signs or symbols on horizontal lines, and written from left to right. They were originally made of crude clay, and partially or wholly baked in the conflagrations which destroyed the palace of Cnossos, being thus preserved virtually intact. Most of them are elongated in shape, but some are rectangular; and the excavators soon found that they could be divided into two classes, according to the signs or symbols with which they were covered:

1. Those with signs which Evans classed as 'Linear A'.
2. Those with signs which he classed as 'Linear B'.

There are far fewer 'Linear A', and a superficial examination revealed that the 'Linear B' script was derived from 'Linear A', being a development or refinement of the latter. Unfortunately, there are not enough 'Linear A' tablets for a definitive interpretation; the exiguous material does not permit of the *internal analysis* which Ventris accomplished for 'Linear B'.[1] But before examining the B tablets, we should remember that A tablets have since been found in all the Cretan palaces which have so far been excavated. But none have been found outside the great island of Minos—a freak of distribution which, we shall see, played an important part in Ventris's decipherment.

Evans unearthed more than 3,000 tablets at Cnossos; they were covered with some eighty different signs, exclusive of ideograms and numerical signs which could easily be identified. A script which employs eighty signs cannot possibly be phonetic; the human throat

---

polation, of which Victor Berard (*Od.*, *loc. cit.*, ed. Guillaume Budé) was already clearly aware (in spite of George Huxley's assertion in *Crete and the Luwians*, Oxford, 1961, p. 43).

[1] Dare we hope that excavations in the new palace discovered by Professor Platon at the extreme eastern end of Crete, at Kato-Zagro (now being excavated), may fill this void? The hope is not unjustified, for the palace was destroyed before 1500 B.C. by an earthquake, and the site not reinhabited.

cannot emit so many elementary and identifiable sounds. Nor can such a script be ideographic, for the number of signs would then be insufficient. The writing is therefore almost certainly syllabic—a deduction endorsed by the analogy between 'Linear B' and a syllabic Greek script found on the neighbouring island of Cyprus. This Cypriot syllabic writing (which we shall later examine in detail) contains about sixty signs, and has been legible since 1870, when its phonetic and grammatical character was elucidated, thanks to the discovery of a bilingual inscription.

Evans took great pains in trying to decipher 'Linear B', but to no avail; this caused him to delay the publication of most of his tablet discoveries as long as possible. And when he died in 1941 the philologists had still had no access to most of the tablets he had discovered more than forty years before. Further work was made more difficult by the fact that Europe was then at war. In 1939, Blegen had discovered more than 700 of the tablets at Pylos in the Peloponnese; and in 1950 and 1952 Wace discovered about fifty at Mycenae in buildings outside the citadel. Keramopoulos had found twenty-eight stirrup-jars with 'Linear B' inscriptions at Thebes.[1] An earthenware jar similarly inscribed had also been found at Eleusis. From all this it seemed certain that the *lingua franca* of the Hellenic bronze age was written in the 'Linear B' script. What was this language?

Evans and his school reasoned thus. The 'Linear A' script had been found on all the Cretan royal sites—and nowhere else. This must therefore have been the way the 'Minoan' language, spoken in the palaces of the Minoan kings, was written. On the other hand, 'Linear B' undoubtedly derives from 'Linear A'. Moreover the similarity between the ceramics, jewelry and various ornaments found on the Continent, and the same objects found in Crete, is apparent to the most unpractised eye. From this, Evans concluded that the continental and Cretan civilisations must have been identical. He assumed that, as Cretan civilisation was anterior to that of the Continent, the appearance of Minoan objects outside Crete, particularly in Mycenae, could only be the result of Minoan expansion. The Minoans must therefore have conquered the whole of Greece, imposing on it their language, art, customs and their 'Linear B' script (evolved and perfected from their first graphic efforts in 'Linear A').

Although probably of non-Indo-European origin, this Minoan

[1] Recently a complete tablet and some fragments have also been found at Thebes.

language had yet to be identified—a problem which, as already stated, Evans failed to solve himself; but it attracted a number of other philologists, and many theories were adduced. The conclusions of the eminent English archeologist Wace, who was at the time in charge of the Mycenaean excavations, were diametrically opposed to those of Sir Arthur about the Minoan-Achaean relationship. But when he announced them, he was promptly recalled to England (Evans and his millions could not be treated in so cavalier a manner); and it was not until after the great man's death that Wace returned to Mycenae to continue his work which, unfortunately, was incomplete at the time of his death.

II. *The False Analogy*

This then briefly is the background to the situation when the young English architect Ventris undertook the difficult task of deciphering the alphabet. His interest in the 'Linear B' script had been aroused at the age of twelve by one of Evans's lectures. He was only an amateur and felt that the great archeologist's theory must be irrefutable; he therefore supported the pan-Minoan idea wholeheartedly—especially as certain statistical dissimilarities between 'Linear B' and Cypriot seemed to prove that the Greek language could not have been written in 'Linear B', a fact which powerfully reinforced the pan-Minoan theory of Sir Arthur and his school.

We may, at this point, consider some aspects of written Cypriot grammar:

1. It possesses a sign for each vowel—a-e-i-o-u.
2. It possesses a sign for each syllable formed by one of these vowels preceded by one of the following consonants—j-k-l-m-n-p-r-s-t-w-x-z.
3. Only the syllables je, ji, ju, wu, ze, zi, zu, xa, xi, xo, xu are not represented.
4. n is omitted before another consonant.
5. A final consonant forms a syllable by the addition of the letter e.
6. To represent a group of consonants, the same number of syllables are formed by adding the vowel of the following or preceding syllable.
7. k = g = k'h
   p = b = p'h
   f = d = t'h

It is curious that this alphabet was preserved locally until a very late epoch although it was most unsuitable for written Greek, whose phonetic symbols had by that time been in use for centuries. According to the rules above, the word 'anthropos' (man) in this Cypriot syllabic script is written:

a-to-ro-po-se

Many Greek words end with the consonant s, which means that if they are transcribed with the Cypriot syllabic alphabet, the sign or symbol denoting 'se' will often be found at the end of a word.

A glance at Table 1 (opposite page) reveals a similarity between the Cypriot and the 'Linear B' symbols. A closer examination reveals that there are even eight signs common to both alphabets. We have summarised them in the double list on the right of Table 1, the third column of this double list showing the phonetic value in Cypriot of the common symbols. There therefore seems little doubt that the Cypriot writing was an adaptation of 'Linear B', and used for writing Greek with the new symbols. Nor can there be any doubt that those who adapted it retained the eight symbols of 'Linear B' unchanged in their new syllabic alphabet.

Now, among the eight signs common to both alphabets is the one representing 'se' phonetically in Cypriot (the fourth in Table 1). In Cypriot inscriptions this sign is often found at the end of a word, as befitting an alphabet that is used for writing Greek. But in the inscriptions on the B tablets the sign is hardly ever found at the end of a word. Moreover, 'Linear B' has no other sign which is used at the end of a word sufficiently often for it to represent the Cypriot 'se'—which invalidates the hypothesis that the 'se' in Cypriot might have changed phonetically when changing alphabets. If this were true, another sign would have replaced it in 'Linear B' (and if 'Linear B' was used for Greek, this new sign would have had the same distribution in B inscriptions as the sign 'se' in Cypriot). But there is no such sign. This total absence of similarity appears to prove statistically that 'Linear B' could not have been used for writing Greek.

Thus the probability that 'Linear B', as a perfected form of 'Linear A', was used for writing Minoan was endorsed by the lack of similarity, or *analogy*, between the Cypriot and the B endings. Moreover it now seemed probable that Minoan was of non-Indo-European origin and again, owing to the lack of *analogy*, that Sir Arthur's pan-Minoan theory was probably correct.

TABLE 1

	1	2	3	4	5
1					
2					
3					
4					
5					
6					
7					
8					
9					
10					
11					
12					

The Linear B script

	a	e	i	o	u
x					
j					
k					
m					
n					
p					
l					
r					
s					
t					
w					
z					

The Cypriot script

B	Cyp.	Val. Cyp.
		ta
		lo
		to
		se
		pa
		na
		ti
		u

Common signs

The problem had now developed to this point. Given the 80-odd symbols of 'Linear B', and given the phonetic values which can be attributed to 8 (some maintain 20) of them by similarity or *analogy* with the Cypriot script—what language, preferably of non-Indo-European origin, could have employed 'Linear B'? In other words, what language can give stable phonetic values to the remaining signs of B? Every known language was tested, sometimes with ludicrous deductions. Ventris himself opted for Etruscan at one point—but only until the summer of 1952. Philologists now began to despair of a solution, and some thought that the Minoan language must have been *sui generis*, and must have vanished completely with the destruction of that people.

III. *The True Analogy*

In a series of articles written between 1943 and her premature death in 1950, Alice Kober, a Brooklyn American, pointed out that all the discernible special characteristics of 'Linear B' should be classified first. Conclusions could then be drawn *by analogy* between these characteristics and the structure of the transcribed language. The quest for phonetic equivalents of the signs could only be undertaken after this classification had been made, and should then conform to the results obtained. In other words, the *internal analogy* should be analysed before the *external analogy*. This perhaps seems obvious now; but no one had thought about it in this way at the time.

The B tablets are almost all inventories of objects which are often identifiable thanks to the way in which the ideograms are placed. The numerical system, which had already been correctly read by Evans, is simple; the words are separated by a small vertical stroke. Kober started her classification of the tablets by examining recognisable ideograms—hence the inventories of chariots, weapons, animals, human beings, furniture, etc. She then found that, in any one category, certain series of signs always followed one another in the same order, to form the same word, with the exception of the last, and sometimes the last two, signs. By *analogy* with other languages, she came to the important conclusion that the language written in 'Linear B' must have been an inflected language.

Let us take Latin as an example, limiting it to the second declension. Writing syllabically, we have:

Ho-me-ru-s	do-mi-nu-s	Ro-mu-lu-s
Ho-me-ru-m	do-mi-nu-m	Ro-mu-lu-m
Ho-me-ri	do-mi-ni	Ro-mu-li
Ho-me-ro	do-mi-no	Ro-mu-lo

As 'Linear B' writing is certainly syllabic, and as all known syllabic writing forms syllables of the 'consonant-vowel' *open* variety, and never the reverse, we may draw two important conclusions from the table above:

1. The variation of symbols in one column (on the basis of our Latin example),

ru	nu	lu
ri	ni	li
ro	no	lo

correspond to one consonant connected with different vowels.

2. The variation of symbols in one line (on the basis of our Latin example),

ru	nu	lu
ri	ni	li
ro	no	lo

correspond to one vowel connected with different consonants.

Now, among the words considered by Kober composed of identical signs (with the exception of the last, or last two, signs), is the inventory or list on page 114 (Table 2). This list has become famous as the 'Kober triplets'.

Each column clearly shows an inflection which is quite independent of the phonetic value attributed to the signs themselves; and the identity of the terminal signs is clear in each line. If we assume that the 'Linear B' syllables are of the usual 'consonant-vowel' form, the *internal analogy* allows us to suppose that the signs of the line A of Table 2 comprise the same vowel coupled to different consonants; and the same can be said for the signs of line B, the vowel forming the syllables of line A being different from the vowel forming the syllables of line B. In this case, each of the pairs of letters shown on the line C of this table include the same consonant coupled to a different vowel.

This *double analogy* may be systematized as in scheme D of Table 2. It was scheme D which served, in fact, as the basis for Ventris's decipherment.

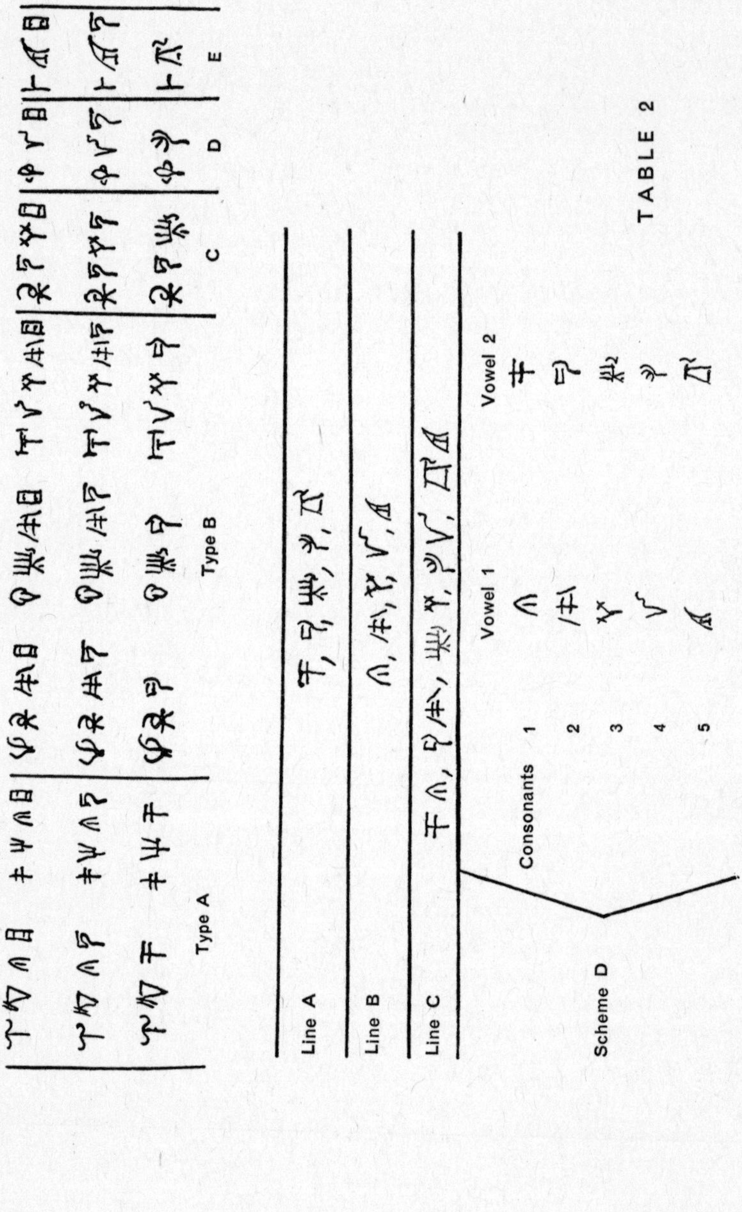

Type A

Type B

C

D

E

Line A

Line B

Line C

Scheme D

Consonants

	Vowel 1	Vowel 2
1		
2		
3		
4		
5		

The Kober Triplets

TABLE 2

On grounds of economy (it is very expensive to print 'Linear B' signs), we cannot follow the long and patient labours of that indefatigable researcher step by step. Working on a basis which forbade him to look for *exterior analogies*, he voluntarily limited his efforts to *interior analogies*. In spite of the difficulties presupposed by such a premise, he gradually succeeded in extending Kober's table (scheme D of Table 2) in both directions, including in it most of the signs composing the 'Linear B' script. He based his research on the following assumptions.

Thanks to the ideograms depicting a man and a woman, Ventris could make use of *analogies* deriving from masculine and feminine inflections. Thanks to the ideograms of the chariot and different weapons, he could add those of neuter origin. Thanks to the signs for figures, he could superimpose on these three cases inflections originating from the singular and plural. This gave six different *analogies* to identify in the terminations of words. He even succeeded in isolating the inflections which, according to him, corresponded to the nominative, genitive, and to a prepositional case. There was also a composite word of two signs which was always interposed between the entries and the corresponding numerical notation, and which probably meant 'total', or 'such a quantity'. This word could also be feminine, masculine or neuter; it could be singular or plural, depending on whether the list comprised a single entry, or several. Lastly, there were two words, each also composed of two signs, whose meaning depended upon the ideogram which accompanied them: man and woman. They too could be in the singular or plural, and enabled the masculine form and the feminine form of the same word to be determined.[1]

[1] We can even deduce from the forms 'man' and 'men' rules 3 and 10 of Mycenaean grammar which we shall examine later. In effect, Cowley had already supposed: Man = korwos = kouros, and Men = korwoi = kouroi. Now, the two words *Korwos* and *Korwoi* are written in 'Linear B' with exactly the same signs. From which we can deduce the two following rules of Mycenean grammar. First, the 's' is omitted at the end of a word; second, the 'i' of the diphthongs is not written (at least at the end of a word). With these two conventions, it is clear that *Korwos* and *Korwoi* are written with the same two signs.

But before the summer of 1952, instead of deducing these grammatical rules from these script-characteristics, Ventris concluded from the identity of the signs for 'man' and 'men' that the written language could only be non-Indo-European. His theory therefore remained in the framework of the *false analogy*.

All these considerations enable new inflections to be isolated, and new signs to be added, by *analogy*, to Kober's table.

This long, detailed and patient work finally brought Ventris in the middle of 1952, still relying only on *internal analogies*, to Table 3 (p. 117). At this time he thought that Minoan, which he identified with Etruscan, was the language of 'Linear B'. But all his efforts were in vain.

He therefore now permitted himself certain *exterior analogies*.

1. He identified the sign of the double axe with 'a', because his statistical tables showed that this sign appeared most frequently at the beginning of words, and that in *all* the known languages 'a' is the most frequent initial sound.

2. He regarded the consonant 12 of Table 3 as 'r' or 'l'. The reasons for this identification are not very clear, but the *analogy* with the Cypriot writing for the termination in 'tro' = to-ro and 'tri' = ti-ri must have influenced him.

3. ia, ja is the feminine ending in Greek, Lycian and Etruscan. Line 1 of Kober's triplets appears to point to similar endings. The third vowel would then have been 'i' which gave, for the sign corresponding to the consonant 14, the phonetic value ti of the Cypriot syllabic alphabet. *Analogy* certainly played a part again here.

4. If jo (consonant 5, column 4) corresponds to the long genitives, then 'o' would be the fourth vowel and 'e' the second. By elimination, 'u' then becomes the fifth.

By employing these hypotheses derived from *exterior analogies* (principally Cypriot), Ventris tried in June 1952 to transcribe the first five of Kober's triplets. Replacing the unknown consonants by the number of the line in the provisional Table 3 in which the transcribed sign figures, we have:

L.-6i-14i-ja	9a-2i-14i-ja	. .-li-13i-ja	60-80-13i-ja	A-7i-8i-13i-ja
L.-6i-14i-jo	9a-2i-14i-jo	. .-li-13i-jo	60-80-13i-jo	A-7i-8i-13i-jo
L.6i-140	9a-2i-140	. .-li-130	60-80-130	A-7i-8i-130

This was the key to the solution. It does not require great knowledge to see that by making

6 = k. 7 = m. 8 = n. 9 = p. 13 = s. 14 = t,

the lower line of Kober's triplets gives the names of the five most important towns of Crete—the top line the feminine plural adjective;

TABLE 3

	a?	e?	i?	o?	u?
1	[illegible]			[illegible]	
2	[illegible]	[illegible]	[illegible]		
3	[illegible]			[illegible]	
4	[illegible]	[illegible]			
5	[illegible]	[illegible]	[illegible]	[illegible]	
6	[illegible]	[illegible]		[illegible]	
7	[illegible]	[illegible]	[illegible]	[illegible]	
8	[illegible]	[illegible]	[illegible]	[illegible]	
9	[illegible]	[illegible]	[illegible]		[illegible]
10		[illegible]		[illegible]	[illegible]
11	[illegible]		[illegible]		[illegible]
12	[illegible]	[illegible]	[illegible]	[illegible]	[illegible]
13	[illegible]	[illegible]	[illegible]	[illegible]	
14		[illegible]	[illegible]	[illegible]	[illegible]
15	[illegible]	[illegible]	[illegible]	[illegible]	[illegible]
?		[illegible]	[illegible]		

Ventris's tentative grid

the middle line, the masculine plural adjective, derived from the names of five towns, namely:

Luktiai	Phaistiai	Tulisiai	Knosiai	Amnisiai
Luktioi	Phaistioi	Tulisioi	Knosioi	Amnisioi
Luktos	Phaistos	Tulisos	Knosos	Amnisos

But the influence of Evans still lingered, so decisively that when Ventris published his findings he stated that the *analogies* he had discovered between the Greek and Kober's triplets were fortuitous—because they relied on the inadmissible premise that the final 's' in words was not transcribed at all.

Why the rule: word + s = word + se (Cypriot) should be admissible; and the rule: word + s = word + nothing (Linear B) should be inadmissible, does not seem evident. But the prejudice was deep-seated.

All the same, the conclusion was now inevitable. By the simple mechanical application of the names of the five Cretan towns to the provisional Table 3, thirty-one of its signs now had phonetic equivalents. Ventris[1] immediately realised that, with their help, a host of words and phrases on many of the tablets could now be read. There could be no further doubt; the language of 'Linear B' had been Greek.[2] After long and arduous work, Ventris had dissolved the spectre of Evans's theories—in which Wace had never believed.

To the unbiased mind the problem was basically non-existent—the kind of false problem which exists because it has not been properly stated.[3]

Script A is found in all the Minoan sites—and only there.

[1] Ventris was killed in a motor accident on 6 September 1956. Born 12 July 1922, he was therefore just 34.

[2] For the non-specialist, the basic work is: John Chadwick, *The Decipherment of Linear B*, Cambridge, 1958. For those who wish to go further the basic work is: Michael Ventris and John Chadwick, *Documents in Mycenaean Greek*, Cambridge, 1956.

[3] Table 1 shows on the left the table of principal signs of the 'Linear B' script. We have deliberately left a gap after the figures, numbering the columns as well as the lines. For the columns, under 1, put a; under 2, put e; under 3, put i; under 4, put o; under 5, put u.

For the horizontal lines, put d after 1, j after 2, k after 3, m after 4, n after 5, p after 6, q after 7, r after 8, s after 9, t after 10, w after 11 and z after 12.

In this way we obtain the table of Mycenaean letters which can be compared directly with the Cypriot symbols of the neighbouring table.

Script B is found throughout the entire Achaean empire. If *a priori* theories are avoided, it is therefore probable that:

Minoan was written in A
Achaean was written in B

And this fits in well with what we know. We may note that Homer had a good deal to say about the language spoken by the Achaeans, insisting that it was the Achaean Agamemnon, and not some Phoenician or Minoan, who lived at Mycenae. He also tells us that Idomeneus, the Achaean, took eighty 'black vessels' from Cnossos to Troy, to take part in the siege. It was therefore the Achaeans who had conquered Crete at the time of the Trojan war (1250 B.C.), and not the Cretans who conquered Greece. This explains why tablets A and B are found at Cnossos—the second corresponding to the Achaean occupation; and also why in continental Greece there are no A tablets. The Cretans never made any conquests on the mainland.

The rules of Cypriot grammar have been given above. It now remains to give those of Mycenaean grammar, in order to compare the two systems. The grammar of 'Linear B' obeys the following rules:

1. There is a sign for each of the vowels a, e, i, o, u.
2. The diphthongs au, eu, ou are indicated by the two distinct corresponding signs.
3. The diphthongs ai, ei, oi, ui omit the i except before a vowel, when this i become j. The initial ai is indicated by the two corresponding signs, except if followed by a vowel.
4. i before a vowel becomes ij.
5. u before a vowel becomes uw; this w corresponds to the digamma of archaic Greek.
6. There is a sign to denote each syllable, of the 'consonant-vowel' form, which can be formed with the five vowels referred to above, and with the consonants: d, j, k, m, n, p, q, r, s, t, w, z; but the syllables ji, ju, qa, qu, wu and zi do not exist.
7. r = l[1].
8. k = g = k'h/p = b = p'h/t = t'h.
9. q = k(w), g(w), k(w)h, and, according to the position it occupies, appears in Greek as k, p, t.
10. The final consonants (n, r, s) are omitted.

[1] This rule, which may seem strange, is less so for those who have lived in Greece. Still today, the people say indiscriminately Aderphos or Adelphos for 'brother', Bourgaros or Boulgaros for Bulgare, etc.

11. The consonants l, m, n, r, s are, inside a word, omitted before another consonant.[1]
12. The initial s is omitted before another consonant.
13. The consonants d, k, p, q, t are indicated before another consonant by separating them from this consonant with the vowel of the following syllable. In this way, they form a supplementary syllable. The same can be said for the combination of the two consonants mn.[2]
14. In addition to the signs in Table 1, a certain number of signs which appear to have been orthographic variants exist.

The *analogy* between Cypriot grammar and that of 'Linear B' writing is now clear, but this does not imply identity—far from it. The only terminal consonants of Greek are n, r, s, which, if in a terminal position in Cypriot, are transcribed as ne, re, se. 'Linear B' omits them: and it is due to this minute detail, responsible for the *false analogy*, that the above Pan-Minoan theory was formulated, and two generations of philologists were deprived of the great contribution which the elucidation of Greek writing in the bronze age would have contributed to our knowledge of antiquity.

This disastrous *false analogy* was more subtle than appeared at first sight. It was not the *analogy* between the appearance and the phonetic value of signs common to Cypriot and 'Linear B' (Table 1) which was false; it was the arbitrary and implicit conclusion that the grammars of these two scripts must be identical. If we refer to the table (1) of signs common to the two scripts, and replace them by their respective phonetic values, we have:

	Cypriot	*Linear B*	
	u	sa	
(In Cypriot t = d)	ta	da	
	ro	lo	(In Mycenaean r = l)
	to	to	
	se	se	
	pa	pa	
	na	na	
	ti	ti	

[1] This is the most inconvenient rule, which can lead to much confusion. For instance, the word ka-ko may belong to the family of words meaning 'bad'; but it can also belong to the k'halko(s) family, meaning 'bronze'.

[2] Thus A-mi-ni-so = Amnisos, and Pa-i-ti-ja = Phaistiai, as in the Kober triplets analysed above.

We see therefore that, except for the first sign, the seven others retain their phonetic value from one script to the other; and even for the first sign error was hardly possible—for if *u* becomes *sa*, a sign representing a vowel is not employed morphologically as a sign representing a syllable in syllabic writing.

The basis established by the phonetic identity of signs common to the Cypriot and Mycenaean alphabets was much broader than that employed by Ventris, principally because, by chance, these identical signs permit the placing of the five vowels from the outset. Starting from the evidence of identical signs, and of historical evidence in the poems of Homer and Hesiod, much of the enormous effort expended on reading 'Linear B' by *internal analogy* only could have been spared.

The exact equation was:

1. A 'Linear B' sign identical with a certain sign in Cypriot syllabic writing retains the identical phonetic in the two scripts.

2. The grammar of 'Linear B' is *analogous to* the grammar of the Cypriot syllabic script.

As a result of the error in replacing the word *analogous* (in point 2 immediately above) by the word *identical* in point 1, the philologists who attempted to decipher 'Linear B' complicated the problem immensely. The problem seemed for long insoluble, owing to the *false analogy* which was based on the different way in which the sign *se* was employed in the two scripts, a minor point in retrospect.

Notes and References

CHAPTER I: PROBLEMS OF CHRONOLOGY

1. In this chapter I shall not give full references for my chronological conclusions. This would lead the reader too far afield. But as the following chapters contain detailed historical accounts of the dynasties briefly catalogued here, I shall, in the course of them, return to all my more controversial points and enlarge on them more specifically, documenting and discussing the relevant sources as required.

2. See especially Prof. D. L. Page, *History and the Homeric Iliad* (University of California Press 1959), Ch. VI: 'Mycenean Relics in the *Iliad*'.

3. It may be of interest to note that the two men who, apart from Evans, contributed most to our knowledge of the Greek Bronze Age were neither archaeologists nor classical scholars: Schliemann was an indigo merchant, and Ventris an architect.

4. The equation of the *akhkhijawā* mentioned in the Hittite archives with our 'Achaeans' is now admitted by most classical scholars. See Page, *op. cit.*, Huxley, *Achaeans and Hittites* (Oxford 1960), G. S. Kirk, *The Songs of Homer* (Cambridge 1962), *et al.*

5. Strabo, 1.2.9: 'Homer took the Trojan War, which was a historical fact, and overlaid it with fantastic tittle-tattle of his own.'

6. Hesiod, *Works and Days* 150–155: 'The weapons of these men were bronze. and bronze their houses,/ and they worked as bronzesmiths. There was not yet any black iron./ Yet even these, destroyed beneath the hands of each other,/ went down into the moldering domain of cold Hades;/ nameless;/ for all they were formidable black death/ seized them, and they had to foresake the shining sunlight.' (Trs. Richmond Lattimore.) Hesiod does not regard the Greeks who lived at the time of the Trojan War as having belonged to the Bronze Age: he describes them separately, in a section immediately following (*loc. cit.* vv. 156–173.)

7. The famous reference to the Dorians in the *Odyssey* is, as we shall see later, almost certainly a late interpolation.

8. In one passage of the *Iliad* (6.168f.) Homer makes an unmistakable allusion, apropos Bellerophon, to some sort of writing. This is almost certainly a memory, preserved through the Dark Ages, of a time when people could send one another written messages—though the contents of the letter entrusted to Bellerophon must have been highly complex for expression in Linear B characters.

9. A. J. B. Wace's Foreword to *Documents in Mycenean Greek*, by Michael Ventris and John Chadwick (Cambridge 1956) p. xxviii.

10. Thucydides 1.10.5f.

11. This is why, at that epoch, sea-borne invasion as distinct from piracy was very difficult. Boats had to be drawn up the beach every night, and water and fodder had to be found. In hostile country this was practically impossible.

12. L. R. Palmer, *Myceneans and Minoans* (Oxford 1961). Even Mylonas, who published a violent attack on Palmer in *Hesperia,* Vol. 31/3, 1962, agrees with his proposed date-scheme.

13. In particular, I regard the arguments used to refute this date-scheme by Huxley (*Crete and the Luwians,* Oxford 1961, p. 50) and G. S. Kirk (*The Songs of Homer*, p. 6, n. 1) as being far too summary to discredit Palmer's solid and detailed thesis. Linguists on the whole seem to accept Palmer's postulation of a Luwian invasion while rejecting his chronology; archaeologists appear to accept his chronology, while rejecting the idea of a Luwian invasion in the Middle Helladic period.

14. The date 1405 corresponds very closely with that of 1410, given by the Parian Marble as the *floruit* of the most ancient Minos—or, in other words, the first Greek King of Crete. I shall give detailed arguments in support of this statement later.

15. At Phaestos the Greek stratum was destroyed during the initial excavation, and no definite pronouncement is possible.

16. G. E. Mylonas, *Ancient Mycenae* (London 1957).

17. C. W. Blegen, *A Companion to Homer,* ed. A. J. B. Wace and F. H. Stubbings (London 1962), Ch. 13, pp. 362–86; cf. Wace, *ibid.*, pp. 386ff., on Mycenae.

18. See Mylonas's article in *Hesperia,* vol. 31/3 (1962), p. 309 n. 66.

19. C. W. Blegen, *Cambridge Ancient History,* fascicle 'Troy' in revised ed. of Vols I–II (Cambridge 1961).

20. On this subject see Furumark, *The Chronology of Mycenaean Pottery,* (Stockholm 1941), p. 115, n. 2.

21. Homer, *Iliad* 6.222.

22. Pausanias 2.15.4.

23. Mylonas, *Ancient Mycenae,* pp. 35f.

24. Hdt. 2.91.

25. Hdt. 7.150.

26. Hdt. 6.53.

27. Homer, *Iliad* 14.320; Hdt. 6.54.

28. Apollodorus, *Bibl.* 2.2.1.

29. See Huxley, *Crete and the Luwians,* p. 36; Sir Alan Gardiner, *Egypt of the Pharaohs* (Oxford 1961), pp. 168ff.

30. Hesiod fr. 24. *Rzach.*

31. Homer, *Iliad* 19.123.

32. Hdt. 2.145.4.

33. Homer, *Iliad* 19.99.

34. The pottery associated with the remains of the Mycenean wall on the Isthmus can be dated to Late Helladic III B. See the article by Oscar Broneer, in *American Journal of Archaeology,* Vol. 62 (1958), pp. 322ff.

35. See Mylonas, *Ancient Mycenae,* p. 65 n. 22.

36. See Mylonas, *ibid.*, p. 37, and also Wace, *Mycenae* (Princeton 1949), where it is demonstrated that the Lion Gate and the Treasury of Atreus have a common style. Furthermore, there are only three royal tombs at Mycenae dating from the Late Helladic III period. Their comparative (not absolute) chronology is established by Wace, *op. cit.* These tombs may be identified with the various local dynasties in the following manner, according to our date-scheme: Tomb of the

Genii—Tomb of the Perseids; Treasury of Atreus—Tomb of the Pelopidae; Tomb of Clytemnestra—Tomb of Aegisthus and Clytemnestra.

37. Pausanias II, 18.8.9.

38. Hdt. 9.26.

39. This change of residence can be explained (see below, Ch. III) by the religious wars of the period, which are all too seldom taken into account. I shall deal with this point *in extenso* at a later stage of my study.

40. In particular Huxley, *op. cit.*, p. 8.

41. Achaean reconstruction is particularly noticeable at Cnossos and Aghia Triadha.

42. Hdt. 4.147.

43. Hdt. 1.2.

44. Hdt. 1.172.

45. Hdt. 4.147.

46. This fleet was naturally manned only by rower-warriors. It was a military expedition, not an invasion with women, children and livestock.

47. Homer, *Iliad* 2.646.

48. Homer, *Iliad* 13.361.

49. *Vide* n. 243.

50. Homer, *Iliad* 13.480.

51. Hdt. 4.147. [This is the island now known as Santorini.—Trs.]

52. L. Palmer, *The Times*, July 17, 1964.

53. Hdt. 5.58–59.

54. *Vide* inscribed jars found by Keramopoulos and the B tablets just brought to light by Dr N. Platon.

55. Euripides, *Phoen.* 8: this conflicts with the evidence of the *Bacchae* (also by Euripides) 213, where Cadmus declares that Pentheus, his grandson by Echion and Agave, is his sole heir. But the *Bacchae* may well be a purely imaginary tale.

56. Euripides. *loc. cit.*; Sophocles, *O.R.* 224.

57. Hdt. 5.59. If one prefers to follow the myth preserved by Herodotus than the one preserved by the tragedians, then the King during the reign of whom the Cadmeans were driven out of Thebes by the Argives (Achaeans) was Laodamos, son of Eteocles (Hdt. 5. 61). But because of the late date that must, as we have seen, be attributed to the birth of Eteocles, this form of the myth presents certain difficulties and the reign of Laodamos must have started when he was still a child, an exceptional event in the bronze age epoch.

58. Thuc. 1.12.3.

59. I have not succeeded in reconstructing the Athenian dynasty. The Athenians played a secondary role during the bronze-age and compensated for it by numerous interpolations in the homeric poems done during the classical period. They also favoured a proliferation of myths from which it has seemed impossible to me to extract the historical "substratum".

CHAPTER II: THE PERIOD BEFORE 1400

60. J. Kaskey published the results of his field-excavation at Lerna between 1952 and 1958 in *Arch. Rev.*, Vol. 29 (1960), pp. 285ff. Lerna III was destroyed by fire during Early Helladic II, and the invaders responsible then built Lerna IV,

which lasted till the Middle Helladic period. At this point Lerna V appears, but there is no violent break with the remains of the previous site. Here we begin to find pottery painted in matt colours, and the custom of burying the dead *intra muros*. Kaskey concludes from this (?) that both Minyan Ware and the use of the potter's wheel have their origin in Early Helladic III.

61. In particular L. R. Palmer, *Myceneans and Minoans* (London 1961), p. 248.

62. W. K. C. Guthrie, *Cambridge Ancient History*, revised ed. of Vols I and II (Cambridge U.P. 1961), fascicle 'The Religion and Mythology of the Greeks', p. 7.

63. See in particular Mellaart, *Anatolian Studies*, Vol. 7 (1957), p. 73; and *Amer. Journ. Arch.*, Vol. 62 (1958), p. 26. Minyan ware is a highly individual type of pottery, generally grey, without decoration and designed to resemble metal.

64. See Palmer, *op. cit.*, Ch. VII, *passim*.

65. Mellaart, *loc. cit.*: this scholar was responsible for excavating Beycesultan.

66. Despite the objections raised by Mylonas in *Hesperia*, Vol. 31 (1962), p. 287.

67. At Cnossos: see Evans, *Palace of Minos*, Vol. 2, p. 309.

68. See D. Perdrizet, *Fouilles de Delphes*, Vol. V, pp. 1–5.

69. See Doro Levi, *Parola del Passato*, Vol. 71 (1960), p. 121.

70. See T. W. Allen, W. R. Halliday, E. E. Sikes, *The Homeric Hymns* (2nd ed., Oxford 1936), pp. 261–2.

71. Huxley, *op. cit.*, 6, pp. 24–7.

72. It is also very likely that the earliest Luwian settlements at Delphi have not been discovered—or disappeared during the famous series of earthquakes which played such havoc with the site.

73. See in particular Mylonas's *Ancient Mycenae*: his arguments are recapitulated in his *Hesperia* article. Wace and Blegen have also often stressed this continuity.

74. See in particular Palmer, *op. cit.*, p. 163, who also cites other scholars as supporting such a view.

75. See Guthrie, *op. cit.*, p. 21, for a refutation of Nilsson's objections to this hypothesis.

76. See M. E. L. Mallowan, *Iraq* (1947), pt. II, p. 184, where a full bibliography of the topic is given.

77. See *inter alia* Stylianou Alexiou, *The Minoan Goddess with Uplifted Hands* (Heracleion 1958).

78. See esp. *The Chronology of Mycenean Pottery* (Stockholm 1941).

79. Hesiod, *Works and Days*, 160ff. (trs. Richard Lattimore).

80. But A is found inscribed on cult objects, B seems to have been strictly utilitarian.

81. The numerous A tablets found by Dr N. Platon in his excavations at Kato-Zagro, not having been baked, are difficult to use as evidence.

82. Modern Greek is a blending of words with Greek, Italian, Turkish and Albanian roots. This language, *malliare*, reflects exactly the recent history of Greece, and to draw a parallel between the situation in A.D. 1960 and 1400 B.C. does not seem absurd.

83. If we do not accept Palmer's chronology, the Cnossos tablets are almost two centuries older than those found at Pylos.

84. Ventris and Chadwick, *Documents in Mycenean Greek* (Cambridge 1956).

85. L. Palmer, *Mycenaean Greek Texts* (Clarendon Press, Oxford, 1963).

86. On this point see Kirk, *The Songs of Homer,* pp. 24f., cf. D. L. Page, *op. cit.,* p. 190 *et seq.*

87. Ventris and Chadwick, *op. cit.,* pp. 72–3.

88. We must surely give up Wace's fine dream of one day discovering a tablet inscribed—in Linear B—with lines from a poet-ancestor of Homer's (see *Documents,* p. xxix). In a personal communication Professor Palmer has informed the present writer that he regards *all* Linear B words as an extremely archaic form of Greek. This would imply that the Luwian language disappeared completely when the two races intermingled. This cannot be ruled out, but seems to me somewhat improbable.

89. The extreme positions on Troy are presented, with all relevant arguments, by both Page and Palmer, in the works cited above.

90. Kirk, *op. cit.,* p. 18, and in particular n. 1, where the reasons for abandoning the theory of a 'Nordic invasion' are set out in detail.

91. See A. R. Burn, *The Lyric Age of Greece* (London 1960), p. 18, for a discussion of the value of such sites. Cf. Pausanias 3.2.1; 7.18.5.

92. Thuc. 1.9.2.

93. Burn, *ibid.*

94. The problem of the *Tsopanis* (nomad shepherd) still remains unsolved in modern Greece.

95. An excellent, if occasionally anachronistic, account of domestic animals in early Greece is given by K. F. Vickery's *Food in Early Greece* (Urbana 1936).

96. By 1600 burials in jars had become rare.

97. The completely evolved "tholoi" are of a lower date.

98. See Mylonas, *ad loc.*, who has a full discussion of these finds, with reproductions.

99. Thuc. 1.3.5.

100. See e.g. *Odyssey* 14.86, 16.425, etc.; cf. H. A. Ormerod, *Piracy in the Ancient World* (Liverpool 1924), and Lionel Casson, *The Ancient Mariners* (London 1959), esp. pp. 167, 199, 201.

101. Thuc. 1.4.

102. Plutarch, *Vit. Thes.* 19.4.

103. Cf. R. W. Hutchinson, *Prehistoric Crete* (London 1962).

104. On the internationalisation of Mycenean art see T. B. L. Webster, *From Mycenae to Homer* (London 1958), pp. 27ff.

105. The great 'Palace Style' jars found in the beehive tombs are all of local origin, and it may be, as Wace remarks (*Documents* p. xxiii), that this may be the ultimate source of their influence on Cnossos. The excavations at present taking place on the far eastern tip of Crete, near Kato Zagro, might make it necessary to revise this opinion. The archaeologist conducting the dig, Dr Platon, has discovered a palace which would seem to have been destroyed by an earthquake *c.* 1500 and never reoccupied. It contains 'Palace Style' vases. But we must wait for the excavation to be completed before pronouncing judgment with any certainty.

106. A. Furumark, The Chronology of Mycenaean Pottery (Stockholm 1941).

107. Thuc. 1.2.5: he calls it *leptógeōn,* 'thin-soiled'.

108. Page, *op. cit.,* p. 171 and n. 72 *ad loc.*

109. The sunken cyst-type tomb is rare outside the Argolidian plain.

110. The phenomenon is even more striking in Egypt.

111. Thuc. 1.11.

112. By far the best edition of *Digenis Akritas* is that by John Mavrogordato (Clarendon Press, Oxford, 1956). The very full introduction is equally perceptive on the poem's origins and MS. tradition. The editions by Legrand and Kalonaros are far more literary in emphasis, and correspondingly less worthy of recommendation.

113. The Danaans in 1400 had been six generations in Greece, and seem to have become totally Hellenised.

114. See e.g. *Documents* No. 11a, Pylos Eo 224. Homer does not use the word *doulos* = bond man but only the word *dmôs* = war prisoner. This distinction is of great importance. Neither did the Dorians use the word *doulos* in the sense of slave. In Argos the Dorians called the slaves *Gymnêtes*, in Laconia *Helots*, in Thessaly *Penestai*, in Crete *Aphamiôtai*. The oldest authorities for the masculine *doulos*=slave seem to be the Codes of Gortyn and Aeschylus (*Pers*. 242).

115. See Kirk, *op. cit.*, p. 33.

116. Note the strange interpretation advanced by Page, *op. cit.*, p. 183. Homer does not use the word *doulos* = bond-man for a slave but calls the slave *dinos* = prisoner of war. The Dorians also did not originally use the word *doulos* for slave. In Thessaly they called them *penestai*, in the Argolis *gymnetes*, in Laconia *helots*, in Crete *Aphamiotai*. *Doulos* is an Achaean word which means 'peasant' and it does not reappear with the meaning 'slave' till very much later.

117. See John Chadwick, *The Decipherment of Linear B* (Cambridge U.P. 1958), p. 120.

118. L. R. Palmer, *op. cit.*, p. 115. Similar systems are to be found in other overpopulated corners of the ancient world, in particular Nuzi in Mesopotamia.

119. Hesiod, *Works and Days* 147. According to Hesiod, as we have already noted (n. 79), these Bronze Age people were different from those of the historical era who fought against Thebes 'over the flocks of Oedipus', and joined the expedition to Troy. Once again we see the value attached to livestock during this period.

120. The Pylos tablets, however, date from *c.* 1200. [Somewhat different views on the prevalence of slavery in the Achaean world may be found, e.g. in Chadwick, *Decipherment*, p. 115; Webster, *From Mycenae to Homer*, pp. 110ff., G. M. Calhoun in *A Companion to Homer*, pp. 433f., 441–2, 459f. (Trs.)]

121. See in particular KN 206=Gg. 705; PY 171=UN 718, etc. Apart from numerous articles of jewellery representing bees, we may note that in 1962, at Peristeria near Pylos, Professor Marinatos found six bees made from gold foil, which had been used to decorate a burial garment.

122. See George W. Elderkin, *The First Three Temples at Delphi* (Princeton 1962), pp. 3ff.

123. Virgil, *Georgics* 4.284. Archelaüs calls bees 'the winged offspring of a dead ox'; Varro and Virgil accept this tradition, but it is attacked by Pliny and Columella. See Varro, *Res Rust.* 3.16; Pliny, *N.H.* 11.23; Columella, 9.14.

124. Hesiod, *Theogony* 977.

125. Pindar, *Pyth.* 9.14.

126. The *Etymologicum Magnum* derives *kéntauros* not from *taûros*, but from a combination of *kentéō aûra.*

127. Pausanias 10.5.9.

128. The first temple had been built with branches of laurel, brought from the Vale of Tempe in Thessaly. This indicates the route taken by those first Minoan sailors who came to worship Apollo Delphinios in the Corcyraean grotto on Mt. Parnassus, close to Crisa with its rich tin deposits.

129. See Elderkin, *op. cit.*, p. 13, for the extremely interesting 'resurrection' of Zagreus as depicted by a fifth-century Attic vase-painting.

130. It is also more than possible that the Minoans introduced hydromel in Delphi at the time of the first laurel-branch temple, but this does not affect the subsequent development of the story. It may be of interest to note that the same dependence of the prophetic gift on intoxication is found in the Old Testament (see Micah 2.11). Cf. on this subject George W. Elderkin's study, *Related Religious Ideas of Delphi, Tara and Jerusalem* (Pond-Ekberg Company, U.S.A., 1961), p. 21.

131. See esp. *Bacch.* 283–5.

132. Nevertheless, as we shall have occasion to remark, archaic-type fermented liquors still continued to be drunk during certain religious rituals.

133. Pausanias (1.32.1) tells us that the Alazones of Scythia let their bees follow their herds out to pasture, 'without shutting them in hives.'

134. See Page, *op. cit.*, Ch. II *passim*, for a conspectus of the works dealing with this question. In my own account I follow Blegen's chronology.

135. There is a vast literature on this topic, of which Page (*op. cit.*, Ch. I *passim*) gives a résumé. For the 'bibloys diphtheras' made of skins of goats or sheep and that cannot survive, see Hdt. 5.58, who ascribes this writing material to 'barbaric' populations.

136. C. W. Blegen, *Troy*, Vol. III, pt. 1, p. 33.

137. See e.g. Homer, *Iliad* 18.288–92; 24.543–6.

138. Homer, *Iliad* 4.437.

139. For all this, the reader is recommended to Blegen's monumental monograph *Troy*, his report on the American excavations there; or else to the revised fascicle of the *Cambridge Ancient History* previously cited above.

140. See E. O. James, *The Cult of the Mother Goddess* (London 1959), pp. 128 f.

141. See Mylonas, *op. cit.*, p. 174.

142. In Cyprus troops armed with machine-guns had to be called out to exterminate the goats that were ruining reafforestation work by eating all the young shoots.

143. Dionysus is mentioned twice in the Linear B tablets, and Zagreus—under the form Sakere—seems to be attested by a tablet from Pylos. See Ventris and Chadwick, *Documents*, p. 425. It may not be irrelevant to notice that, except for the small royal chapels, Minoan worship has hardly left any trace. The same is true to an even greater degree of the Mycenaean practice. See Lord William Taylor, *The Mycenaeans* (Thames and Hudson 1964), p. 67.

144. See Wace *Documents* Introduction p. XXI

145. Held, in particular, by Huxley; *op. cit.*, Ch. II, *passim*.

146. Palmer, *op. cit.*, Ch. VI.

147. In particular, the stirrup-jars we find represented on the tablets surely did not exist before 1400 B.C.

148. Huxley, *op. cit.*, Ch. II.

149. One is reminded of the story about the man who was argued into letting himself be guillotined.

150. See the map in Page, *op. cit.*, p. 125.

151. The contrary hypothesis is the equivalent of saying that since Attic pottery is abundant in Etruria, this proves not merely that the Etruscans were fond of Attic pottery, but that the Athenians conquered Etruria.

152. Even A. W. Hutchinson, *Prehistoric Crete* (London 1962), who accepts (e.g. on p. 106) the theory of an Achaean dynasty settled in Cnossos between 1450 and 1400, is finally forced to contradict himself (see p. 269) by admitting that the relief frescoes of this period can only be a purely Cretan development—which obviously excludes the hypothetical Greek dynasty.

153. I shall discuss the circular plan of Tiryns in this connection at a later point.

154. From *hýron*, a beehive.

155. Herodotus, who tells the story (7.170.1), naturally refers to the King of Crete as Minos. For a fifth-century Greek all Kings of Crete were so named. Herodotus adds one interesting detail: the people of Polichné and Praesus, he says, did not take part in the expedition—a statement which archaeological evidence seems to confirm. However, both these localities came back under the aegis of Cnossos, as we see from the Linear B tablets (see *Documents*, p. 141). Herodotus says that Minos set off in pursuit of his architect Daedalus, who had fled the realm. Huxley accepts this quite literally. I find such an explanation unlikely: the great architect's fortification of the Sicilian villages was very probably the cause of the disastrous war that followed.

156. Diodorus Siculus, 4.79.4.

157. *Ibid.* 4.79.3.

158. See L. Bernabo Brea, *Sicily before the Greeks* (London 1957), p. 178.

159 Huxley, *op. cit.*, p. 5 (cf. Vercoutter, 413).

160. The Aegean pottery found in Egypt, of a type belonging to Late Helladic IIIa, is Mycenaean, not Cretan. See Wace and Blegen in *Clio*, Vol. 32 (1939), pp. 145ff.

161. See above, n. 155, about Polichné and Praesus returning to Cnossos.

162. If Palmer's theory of a Luwian invasion of mainland Greece proves correct: *op. cit.*, p. 248 (cf. Ch. VII *passim*).

163. W. K. C. Guthrie, *op. cit.*, p. 9. Dionysus was identified with the ancient Cretan deity whose rites, like his own, were of an orgiastic nature. But the Greeks had already given this god the Indo-European name of Zeus—in a somewhat incongruous fashion—on account of his importance (*ibid.*, p. 3).

164. The question of Palmer's and Evans's rival date-schemes (I propose to follow Palmer's here) still arouses too much emotional heat to permit of its rational discussion on the evidence as it stands. It seems to me there exists one irrefutable method of deciding who is right and who wrong. This involves the *pithoi*, those gigantic Greek and Minoan jars which have certainly never been shifted since their original manufacture. If the Achaeans really took Cnossos in 1405 and continued to exploit it till 1100, it is a foregone conclusion that during those three centuries a certain number of damaged *pithoi* would have had to be replaced. If it could be shown that among the *pithoi* in the store-rooms of Cnossos there existed certain specimens which resembled those found at Pylos and Mycenae—in other words, *pithoi* of Achaean manufacture—then Palmer's theory would be proved beyond all possible doubt.

All archaeologists I have consulted agree upon this point, but no one is willing to embark on such an examination, which would be lengthy, though not intrinsically difficult. From personal observation the author is convinced that among the *pithoi* of Cnossos there do, in fact, exist a certain number *which are not Minoan but Achaean*, and which, more particularly, are identical with the *pithoi* discovered in Pylos. This is why I have employed Palmer's date-scheme rather than that of Evans. (Evans himself, incidentally, in *The Palace of Minos*, Vol. II, p. 689, reproduces a photograph of *pithoi* which, without going into detail, he declares to be of a different period. His text suggests that the picture was taken from the opposite side to that shown by the photograph itself.)

CHAPTER III: THE DAWN OF HISTORY

165. Hdt. 1.2.
166. Homer, *Iliad* 14.321.
167. Homer, *Iliad* 2.646.
168. Euripides, *Phoen.* 6.
169. Hdt. 7.170.1.
170. Pindar, *Ol.* 2.25; Euripides, *Bacchae*; Homer, *Iliad* 14.305; Hesiod, *Theog.* 940.
171. Plutarch, *De Is. et Os.* 35 (365 A), quoting Pindar.
172. Previously the Tyrians had, in all likelihood, depended on palm-wine.
173. See P. E. Newbury, *The Life of Rekhmara* (London 1900), pl. xiii.
174. See *Hesperia*, Vol. 9 (1940), p. 283 and fig. 24. In the absence of written documents the manufacturing of wine in a given region can only be deduced from the appearance in that region of *locally produced* vessels suitable for the preservation and transportation of wine. Prof. G. Mylonas has pointed out to me that remains of grapes have been found in M.H.III vessels, in particular at Aghios Kosmas. But it is a far cry from grapes to wine. We know that dried fruit (probably raisins and figs) was a staple food of the Achaeans. The tablets have a special ideogram to characterise rations of this sort. Anyhow the vessels containing the grapes are quite unsuitable for wine. So are all forms of 'pithoi'. Amphoras with narrow necks, the only ones suitable for storing wine, do not appear to have been made in Greece before L.H.IIIB. See Furumark, *The Mycenaean Pottery*, p. 595, par. 69. This is 150 years later than Canaan amphoras. See *Amphoras*, American School of Classical Studies at Athens (Princeton, New Jersey, 1961), in particular plates 14 and 15.
175. Hdt. 2.49; 5.7.
176. Note the connection between *Boiōtia* and *bous* (an ox).
177. This is why, in the Catalogue of Ships in the *Iliad*, Boeotia takes up nearly one-third of the total space: the Catalogue *only* lists the followers of the bull, who, as we shall see, were setting out in the hope of annihilating the goat-worshippers of Troy altogether.
178. Homer, *Odyssey* 11.262f.
179. I. Threpsiades, *Bulletin de la Société Archéologique* (Athens), issue for May 1961. During the excavations there was found one half of a large double-horn emblem, in limestone, identical to those discovered in Crete. This amply demonstrates—as if further proof were needed—the nature of the cult practised by the Boeotians, who would be naturally hostile to the Cadmean goat-worshippers.

180. Pausanias 9.12.4; Apollodorus, *Bibl.* 3; Ovid *Met.* 3.1ff.

181. Hesiod, *Theog.* 975f.; Pindar, *Pyth.* 9.116.

182. Virgil, *Georg.* 4.331.

183. See esp. Pindar, *Ol.* 2.86.

184. Pausanias 9.12.4.

185. See the publication of the American School of Classical Studies mentioned in note 174.

186. A deep trench divides the enclosure probably in order to separate horses from cattle.

187. See K. Müller, *Tiryns* (1912–39), vol. 1, pp. 205–9. In 1962 the highly complicated system for supplying water to the outer enclosure was discovered.

188. I have been informed that this prepalatial building dates from well before 1600 B.C., but then we can no longer be certain that it is Achaean.

189. See A. D. Keramopoulos in *Bulletin Archéologique*, Vol. 3 (1917), pp. 253ff.

190. See note 52.

191. See J. L. Kaskey in *Hesperia*, Vol. 31/3 (1962), p. 275 and Vol. 33/3 (1964), p. 314. But latest results indicate that the remodelling of the building took place after 1100.

192. By Prof. Marinatos: see S. Iacovides, *L'Acropole mycénienne d'Athènes* (Athens 1962), p. 11.

193. Friedrich Matz, *La Crète et la Grèce primitive* (Paris 1962), p. 183.

194. If this theory is correct it would be tempting to regard the famous gold mask with round eyes (found in Shaft Grave IV at Mycenae and now in the National Museum in Athens) as that of some Cyclopian architect whom the chieftains of the Achaean tribes employed—at that time probably for funerary construction-work—about the end of the sixteenth century. Marinatos, in the introduction to Iacovides's book mentioned above, mentions Cecropians, Almopians and Dryopians. The crushed death mask from grave V (163 in Marinatos' *Crete and Mycenae*) (*Thames and Hudson*) seems to have been a cyclop's mask also.

195. See discussion in note 272.

196. I shall return at a later point to the continued use of hydromel in certain ritual ceremonies.

CHAPTER IV: THE EARLY DYNASTIES

197. Pausanias 10.10.5.

198. *Ibid.* 3.17.6.

199. Cf. Sir J. G. Frazer's edition of Pausanias, Vol. 3, p. 345.

200. Pausanias 3.17.6.

201. Hesiod, *Works and Days* 150. It is well known that the archaic temple of Athena at Sparta was similarly plated with bronze, in part at least.

202. See especially Hesiod, fr. 24, Rzach[3].

203. See Homer, *Iliad* 14.319.

204. Cf. Huxley, *op. cit.*, p. 36.

205. Fr. 21, Jacoby.

206. Being descended from a son of Jacob and Bilhah, one of Rachel's servants: see Genesis 35.25, 46.23; Numbers 26.42.

207. See Judges 5.17.

208. See Furumark, *op. cit.*, pp. 118–22. These episodes concerning the Philistines and their defeat by Rameses III must certainly be linked with the raids made by the 'people of the sea' and their crushing by the same Pharao. These 'people of the sea' must in turn, in all probability, be linked with the Cycladic islands. These islands play a surprisingly small role in Homer, compared with Ithaca, Aegina, Salamis, Rhodes and the twin kingdom of Pheidippus and Antiphus (Calydnae, Cos, Nisyros, Carpathos, Casos). The archaeological evidence is not yet sufficient to prove this link, but excavations have been on a very small scale. These Cycladic islands were avoided by the Greeks as far as possible when sailing to or from Troy. They were no part of the Achaean Empire and probably dangerous ground to tread on. Homer (*Il.* II.723) specifies that the Achaeans abandoned Philoctetes on Lemnos which implies that Lemnos was not Achaean territory. The culture is of a very different nature and easy to distinguish from the Greek. There is no valid reason to think that these islands did not suffer from the same overpopulation problems as the mainland. The homeless took naturally enough to the sea and ravaged the unfortified coast southwards, setting the Philistines in motion till they came up against the Egyptian forces of Rameses III. But to suppose gratuitously that these pirates could besiege Gla or Mycenae (some distance from the coast) and force their enormous fortifications seems to me, wholly unwarranted. As I have stated above I do not believe in large scale sea borne invasions in the bronze age when food was scarce and ships not very seaworthy. The 'people of the sea', like the Philistines, belong entirely to the history of Asia. This is why I have not mentioned them in this book, though some Achaeans (in particular from Cyprus) may well have joined them in their raids.

209. Judges 16ff.

210. *Ibid.* 18.

211. I Kings 12.29.

212. Judges 18.30.

213. This proves that the original tribal location of the Dans must have been by or near one of those small marshy plains at the mouth of some Palestinian river. Mellaart has recently discovered, at Tsatal-Hugiuk in Asia Minor, a genuine city, dating from about 6500 B.C., which contains a sacred edifice—accessible only through its roof, and consecrated to the bull-cult.

214. Which also gave us Cadmus's dates. See n. 52.

215. Cf. Huxley, *op. cit.*, pp. 57–8.

216. Joshua 19.46.

217. Apollodorus, *Bibl.* 2.4.4.

218. Hdt. 2.44.

219. Hesiod, *Shield* 11. I regard the first 54 verses of this late poem as Hesiod's own work. Cf. Paul Mazon's edition (Paris 1951), pp. 119ff.

220. *Ibid.* 11–13.

221. Pindar, *Pyth.* 9.82.

222. Pindar, *Isth.* 1.13: Hesiod, *Shield* 49.

223. Hesiod, *Shield* 34–54; Pindar, *Pyth.* 9.85.

224. Thuc. 1.9.2.

225. So Ephorus 70 (fr. 118, Jacoby).

226. Pindar, *Ol.* 1.113.

227. See the chronological table. Thyestes must have been the younger in order to have reigned, however briefly, in 1260.

228. Asine, which is mentioned with Hermione in Homer, *Iliad* 2.560, is not included among the Danaans' possessions, of which it certainly was one.

229. The date can be no later because of the first Attica campaign of 1285.

230. Homer, *Iliad* 19.90–133.

231. *Ibid.*, 8.362ff.

232. The very interesting symbolism attached to these mythical works would necessitate a special non-historical study.

233. Hdt. 2.41.

234. Hdt. 2.145; cf. above, Ch. I, p. 8 and n. 30 *ad loc.*

235. Although Homer specifies his enmity with the royal house of Pylos. Homer, *Iliad* 11.690. See also Frank H. Stubbins' *The Rise of Mycenaean Civilisation*, Cambridge Ancient History fascicles 1963–64, p. 28.

236. Hdt. 2. 42.

237. Those who do not wish to accept Herodotus's version, and who want to make the Dorians come from Illyria, try to derive the name Hyllus from *Hyllēis polis* in Illyria, though the only authority for this name is Apollonius Rhodius (*Arg.* 4.535), while the Lydian river of the same name is referred to by Homer (*Iliad* 20.392) and Herodotus (1.80). After all, the Achaeans did come from Asia Minor. We might, too, consider the Egyptian fish *hyllos* mentioned by Aristophanes of Byzantium. Amphitryon's ancestors had come from Egypt with the first Dans.

On the Epirot and Illyrian origin of the Dorians see N. G. L. Hammond, *Annual of the British School at Athens*, Vol. 32 (1931/2), pp. 131ff. All these questions of origin only become necessary if we assume that the Dorians were a vast horde. But this is contradicted by the evidence of Herodotus and Isocrates, which I shall examine in due course: there is no testimony which would enable us to challenge their veracity—except a qualified modern theory of a 'Dorian invasion'.

238. Pindar, *Pyth.* 9.80; Pausanias, 1.44.9.

239. The pottery associated with this wall is Late Helladic IIIb, which dates it to slightly later than 1300.

240. Cf. S. Iakovides, *L'Acropole mycénienne d'Athènes* (Athens 1962), p. 208.

241. We do not know Gla's ancient name. The traditional identification with Arné is most improbable. Gla dates from the same period as the first ring-wall round the Acropolis: see Iakovides, *op. cit.*, p. 226.

242. I. Threpsiades in *Bulletin Archéologique* (Athens 1961).

243. The conquest of Rhodes was, as we shall see, forced upon the Achaeans, and not deliberately sought.

244. Naturally this Sarpedon is not the Lycian who fought in the Trojan War: see e.g. *Iliad* 2.876. Chronology forbids any such identification.

245. Ephorus 10 (fr. 117, Jacoby). Professor G. Mylonas has pointed out to me that there existed in Myletus a small native city whose Achaean pottery (imported) dates back to L.H.I. that is *c.* 1500–1450. It is this city that Sarpedon colonised.

246. See Homer, *Iliad* 2.647.

247. See Homer, *Iliad* 2.686.

248. Hdt. 1.173; cf. 7.93.

249. See the *Zeitschrift des Deutschen Morgenländischen Gesellschaft*, Vol. 94 (1940), pp. 209–10.

250. Huxley, *op. cit.*, p. 17, 5; but if we accept my date scheme his conclusions must, of course, be reversed.

251. For the date of the Lion Gate see G. Mylonas, *op. cit.*, 66.

252. The pottery sherds associated with the Isthmus wall are also L.H.IIIb.

253. Homer, *Iliad* 4.390.

254. *Circa* 1265. See the very curious interpretation of F. Vian, *Les origines de Thebes, Cadmos et les Spartes* (Paris, Klincksieck, 1963), p. 236 sq.

255. The list of the seven chieftains who attacked the seven gates of Thebes varies according to our sources. The following list is often adopted: Hippomedon, Tydeus, Parthenopaeus, Polynices, Adrastus, Amphiaraus, and Capaneus. Other sources give Eteocles instead of Adrastus, while the Athenians included their own fellow citizen Peteus. The whole tradition is somewhat confused.

256. See Homer, *Iliad* 4.405.

257. Pindar (*Pyth.* 8.41) specifically states that the Epigoni set out from Argos.

258. Hdt. 5.61.

259. Hdt. 9. 26–7.

260. This distinction is most probably an anachronism.

261. Hdt. 9.27.

262. This passage from Herodotus should be compared with Pindar, *Isthm.* 1.31ff., where the poet makes a distinction between the 'Spartans' (i.e. the descendants of the men who sprang up from the dragon's teeth sown by Cadmus) and the Achaeans who inhabited the high plateaux of Therapnae.

263. See n. 134.

264. Hdt. 5.61.

265. Hdt. 1.56.

266. Dorus (see chronological chart) was the son of Deucalion; if he really was the Cretan prince's descendant, this would in fact date his *floruit*, with some exactness, to the War of the Epigoni.

267. Hdt. 8.31.

268. Andron of Halicarnassus 10 (fr. 16 a–b).

269. Hdt. 7.171.

270. Homer, *Odyssey* 19.177.

271. In the Belles Lettres edition of the *Odyssey*, Victor Bérard regards these two famous lines as an interpolation. I am very willing to accept this hypothesis, since this passage is the only place in all Homer and Hesiod where mention is made of the Dorians: a suspicious circumstance, to say the least of it, and the text reads infinitely better with the two lines excised.

272. This armour can be dated to *c.* 1400. See Prof. Verdelis in *Archaeological Reports for 1960–61* (Council of the Society for the Promotion of Hellenic Studies, 1961), p. 9, and cf. Leonard Cottrell, *The Lion Gate* (London 1963), pp. 104–7 and pl. facing p. 112. The armour bears no resemblance to the equipment portrayed on the Linear B tablets. The cuirass is formed of two single plates, at back and front. It also embodies a kind of bronze baldric and a protective neck-piece, the latter again being made of a single sheet of metal. Three lapping

bronze strips bring it down to knee-level. The development that lies between this ultra-heavy model and the laced corselets of the Linear B tablets is obvious. Palmer is right over this, and Mylonas's refutation in *Hesperia* (*loc. cit.*) lacks cogency. This extraordinary armour will be placed on display in the Argos Museum. See illustration p. 77. The Linear B description of armour is completely different: 'The body was protected by a corselet, the material is not specified but one tablet hints at linen. Attached to this were some thirty or more plates, twenty large and ten small, or in some cases twenty-two large and twelve small.' John Chadwick, *The Decipherment of Linear B* (Penguin Books 1958), p. 110. See also Palmer, *Minoan Greek Texts*, p. 488.

273. There is here an irony: Troy became a danger at a time when she became poor and weak.

274. Homer, *Iliad* 6.57–60.

275. See C. W. Blegen, *op. cit.*, Troy, p. 14.

276. Stesichorus, ed. Bergk, Fr. 11.

277. Euripides, *Helen* 31ff.

278. Homer, *Iliad* 1.348–63, 5.860ff., 18.478–613, 22.62.

279. Homer, *Odyssey* 5.87–91, 7.179, 14.78, 15.148ff., 16.118–299.

280. Cf. Michael Grant, *Myths of the Greeks and Romans* (London 1962), pp. 49–50.

281. Homer, *Iliad* 2.653–71.

282. This Tlepolemus, who was King of Rhodes and the southern Sporades, is also mentioned in a Chian inscription of the third century B.C.: see *Journal of Hellenic Studies* (1954), p. 162.

283. Homer does not tell us the motive for this murder. Apollodorus, *Bibl.* 2.8.2, claims that Tlepolemus killed Licymnius accidentally, while Pindar, *Ol.* 7.27ff., says that he struck him down in a fit of rage.

284. Homer, *Iliad* 2.664–9.

285. Apollodorus, *Bibl.* 2.4.5; Schol. Hom. *Iliad* 19.116; Schol. Apoll. Rhod. *Argon.* 1.474.

286. Plutarch, *Vit. Thes.* 7.

287. Pindar, *Ol.* 7.29; Apollodorus, *Bibl.* 2.4.5.

288. Homer, *Iliad* 2.658; Apollodorus, *Bibl.* 2.7.6; Pindar, *Ol.* 7.24, calls her Astydameia, while Pherecydes, schol. 42b, gives her name as Astygeneia.

289. Homer, *Iliad* 19.116ff.

290. See Page, *op. cit.*, Ch. I, 'Achaeans in Hittite Documents', which summarises the latest research on this question.

291. To link Tlepolemus with the Dorians on account of his Heraclid ancestry is a nonsensical and anachronistic error perpetuated by almost every Greek scholar who tackles the subject. We must adhere strictly to our chronological chart. There was never more than one Heracles, whose *floruit* occurred half a century before the Trojan War; and it was, beyond a doubt, his son Tlepolemus who colonised Rhodes, Lindos, Cameiros and Ialysos, after fleeing his country to avoid a clan vendetta. He was killed by Sarpedon, King of Lycia (Homer, *Iliad* 2.627–98). We only know his successors from their correspondence with the Hittite emperors. Page's theory (*op. cit.*, p. 148) seems debatable. Cf. Pindar, *Ol.* 7.19ff.

292. Homer, *Iliad* 2.679.

293. I.e. Delphi.

294. Homer, *Iliad* 2.519.

295. Homer, *Iliad* 9.404ff. The different epithets used to characterise Pytho and Crisa are, once again, symptomatic. There were tin deposits at Crisa, and divine protection might prove efficacious against some band of corsairs whose superstition outweighed their rapacity.

296. Homer, *Iliad* 2.603–14.

297. For the generally harmful intervention of the gods in the process of human thought see Charles Mugler *Les origines de la science grecque chez Homère*, Paris, Klucksieck 1963, p. 196.

298. See in particular G. S. Kirk, *op. cit.*, pp. 12ff.

299. Homer, *Iliad* 14.249ff.

300. Thuc. 1.9.

301. Thuc. 1.8.4–5.

302. Chadwick, *Decipherment*, p. 119.

303. This must be linked to the splendour of the Orchomenos beehive tomb, the last and most beautiful erected by the Achaeans; new riches were being exploited at that time (after 1240).

304. That perfumed oil was exported in stirrup-jars is one of the more revolutionary conclusions reached by Palmer (*op. cit.*, p. 186), and dates the Cnossos tablets, incontestably, to a period after L.M.IIIb (*circa* 1250). Mylonas (*Hesperia, loc. cit.*, pp. 304ff.) questions Palmer's assertion that the trade in scented oil was a monopoly held by Cnossos. On this point he could well be right, and the so-called 'Oil Merchant's House' in Mycenae turn out to be the local monarch's scented-oil *factory*: the last *pithos* is placed in such a manner that a fire can be lit under it, which lends support to such a theory. Mylonas suggests that the twenty-eight stirrup-amphorae bearing Linear B inscriptions, which Keramopoulos discovered at Thebes, might well be of local manufacture rather than Cretan imports. The problem, alas, cannot be resolved one way or the other. The present writer has discussed it with several archaeological specialists, and all agreed that it was impossible to distinguish between clay from a Theban quarry and clay from the many various Cretan quarries. The only possible distinguishing mark would be some special characteristic in the inscriptions; but in order to have some sure points of reference one would need to conduct extensive excavations at Thebes in the hope of turning up Linear B tablets in sufficient number so as to be able to distinguish a Theban style of writing. Will the excavations actually under way allow us to arrive at such a distinction? For the moment it may seem more prudent to restrict oneself to Palmer's remark: the name in the genitive case upon the jars (indication of origin) seems, in the majority of the vessels, to be a Cretan geographical denomination. The spectrographic sherds-analysis of H. W. Catling, E. E. Richards and A. E. Blin Stoyle (*The Annual of the British School of Athens* No. 58 (1963), p. 109) has rather startlingly confirmed the impossibility of distinguishing Theban from Cretan clay.

305. See Wace, *Mycenae*, p. 114.

306. Chadwick, *Decipherment*, p. 122.

307. Excavations undertaken at Sparta with a view to unearthing Bronze Age settlements have so far proved altogether inadequate. In particular, the palace of Menelaus has not yet been discovered. See the *Bulletin* of the British School of

Archaeology, Vol. 45 (1950), pp. 287–8. For the beehive tombs of Amyclae see H. L. Lorimer, *Homer and the Monuments* (London 1950), p. 254.

308. See Marinatos's introduction to Iakovides, *op. cit.*, p. 17. The Pelargicum's existence is attested by a wide range of ancient sources, in particular by Thucydides, 2.17. For an exhaustive bibliography on the subject see Iakovides, p. 231f.

309. Chadwick, *Decipherment*, p. 112. Although a certain number of these tablets may be interpreted to mean that one horse only is allocated to a particular chariot because it has already got one other.

310. See Page, *op. cit.*, p. 193, for a complete refutation of Palmer and Chadwick on this point. For the date of the destruction of Pylos, see Blegen, *op. cit.*, p. 16.

311. See Mylonas, *op. cit.*, p. 71.

312. Pausanias 2.18.8–9.

313. Hdt. 5.65.

314. Thuc. 1.2.6.

315. See Andrew Robert Burn, *The Lyric Age of Greece* (London, Edward Arnold, 1960), p. 6.

316. Thuc. 1.2.5.

317. Pindar (fr. incert. 116, ed. Puech) describes Theseus's ancestors as going back to Zeus (the bull) and Poseidon (the horse); but the Athenians always sacrificed bulls and lambs together, perhaps thus symbolising the union of the classes. Cf. Homer, *Iliad* 2.460.

318. On the synoecismus see Thuc. 2.15.2ff.

319. Tyrtaeus ap. Strabo 8.362 (Diehl 3 fr. 2): 'For Zeus himself, the son of Cronus, and spouse to fair-wreathed Hera, bestowed this city upon the sons of Heracles; with whom we, leaving windy Erineus, came to the broad isle of Pelops' (i.e. the Peloponnese). For Erineus cf. Thuc. 1.107.2.

320. Hdt. 1.56.

321. *Dōrieùs* is a shortened form of *Dōrímachos*.

322. Isocrates (12.255, p. 76, Blass) asserts that the number of Spartans at the time of their immigration did not much exceed 2000, which seems a reasonable supposition. Cf. G. L. Huxley, *Early Sparta* (London 1962), n. 42, and Thucydides, 1.18.1, who says that the Spartans did not achieve a stable form of government till some four centuries before his own day—which means that the four Dorian settlements of Laconia (Pitana, Mesoa, Limnae and Cynosura) remained at loggerheads with one another till the end of the ninth century. When they first reached Laconia the Dorians were so few in number that between 1150 and 1100 they could not occupy the entire plain, and were forced to leave Amyclae in peace, merely concluding a treaty with her, and thus leaving an Achaean outpost in the very heart of Laconia. (See C. A. Christou's *Archaía Spártē* (Sparta 1960), p. 2.) Nor should we forget the later course of Spartan history, with the country organised like some military camp in a perpetual state of mobilisation—sure indication of their pressing need (if they were not to be destroyed) to defend themselves against the vast majority of the country's inhabitants. Their degree of success in this object can only be accounted for by the population's traditionally unwarlike character. Yet the Dorians took six hundred years to subjugate the neighbouring territory of Messenia, and several times they nearly succumbed as a result of the burden which these campaigns placed on them. If the Achaeans had

been the race of warriors which certain historians try to convince us they were, the course of history would have taken a very different turning.

323. See Oscar Broneer, *Amer. Journ. Arch.*, Vol. 52 (1948), pp. 111–14.

324. Hellanicus, fr. 125 (Jacoby: cf. his remarks *ad loc.*).

325. Homer, *Iliad* 2.547.

326. Thuc. 2.17.

327. Ephorus 70, fr. 121 (Jacoby).

328. Pausanias 2.13.1.

329. *Ibid.* 2.37.3.

330. Wace, *Documents*, Introd. p. xxx.

331. Desborough, *The Last Mycenaeans and their successors* (Clarendon Press 1964). See also L. Palmer's criticism of this book in *The Oxford Magazine*, 11 June 1964, 373.

332. Code of Gortyn, col. 5 lines 25ff.

333. Cf. R. F. Willetts, *Aristocratic Society in Ancient Crete* (London 1955), p. 100, cf. pp. 46–51.

334. Hesiod, *Works and Days* 153.

335. Though here it is more the case of a society whose ruling class had become out of date than of a loss of faith.

CHAPTER V: THE AFTERMATH

336. Hdt. 5.65; Pausanias 7.2.3.

337. The classification of Attic pottery between the years 1120 and 980 is still very unsatisfactory. There are several quite inexplicable gaps in the sequences.

338. Cf. C. Roebuck, *Ionian Trade and Colonisation* (New York 19559), pp. 2ff.

339. Hdt. 1.149.

340. As is made clear by Herodotus's remark concerning the troops who defeated Hyllus at the Isthmus wall: Hdt. 9.26, see n. 237.

341. For a study of the oral tradition see, *passim*, a book frequently cited in these pages: G. S. Kirk's *The Songs of Homer*.

342. Cf. D. L. Page, *op. cit.*, Ch. VI.

343. Cf. T. B. L. Webster, *From Mycenae to Homer* (London 1958), pp. 187ff. The Homeric poems seem to have been the property of a clan or guild, the Homeridae, who gave public recitations of them. See Pindar, *Nem.* 2.5.1.

344. The idea of the 'soldier of Christ' derives from Constantine I; cf. Max Hirmer's *Römische Kaiserporträts im Münzbild* (Munich 1951), p. 24, and the very curious portraits of Constantine the Great which he reproduces.

345. See A. Delatte, *Le Cycéon* (Paris 1955); and Homer, *Iliad* 11.624ff.

346. Homer, *Odyssey* 10.234.

347. See Delatte, *op. cit.*, *passim*.

348. There would seem to be a connection here with the concept of the triad or trinity. Since the Mycenaean era men had always reckoned in threes: this year, last year, next year. This year's harvest is born of last year's, which provides both seed and 'mother' for the harvest of the year to come. But the three harvests form one single entity, i.e. the worshipper's sustenance. Cf. G. W. Elderkin, *Related Religious Ideas of Delphi, Tara and Jerusalem*: A Study of Dionysiac Tradition. (Pond-Ekberg Co., U.S.A., 1961), p. 38.

349. Notwithstanding the fact that in the Roman environment then prevailing the two fertility myths could only be pretexts for literary fashions.

350. According to Plutarch (*De Isid. et Os.* 35, 365A) and Philo (cf. 22j), beside the tripod—which had on it a *hólmos*, a kind of cauldron in which the Pythia sat—there was, in the *adyton* at Delphi, the tomb of Dionysus, with the inscription: *Here lies the body of Dionysus son of Semele.* The initiates (*hósioi*) offered a secret sacrifice at this tomb. Cf. esp. Erwin Rohde, *Psyche*, pp. 14.132. Also in the *adyton*, according to Pausanias (10.24–5), was 'a second golden image of Apollo'. As during his visit Pausanias passed from the *cella* to the *adyton*, this phrase can only mean that he found in the *adyton* a statue of the God different from the *Apollo Moiragétès* which he describes earlier. According to Euripides (*Phoen.* 232), the oracle was delivered in a cave or grotto (*ántron*, *spéleon*); and according to Plutarch (*Vit. Timoleon.* 8) those making enquiries of the oracle were described as '*going down* to the oracular shrine'. Though Pausanias has nothing to say on this point, we may infer from these passages that the *adyton* was at a lower level than the rest of the temple, perhaps in order to simulate the tomb of Dionysus—a point which the excavations conducted by the French School at Athens would appear to have confirmed.

351. The second Greek miracle was, as I have indicated, in a very real sense the child of the first, especially as regards Homeric culture, which permeated it at every level and ended in the absurdities of Heraclitan allegory.

BIBLIOGRAPHY

352. Eur., *Hel.* 148–50, Pind. *Nem. IV* 46–8.
353. Homer, *Iliad* 8.281–5.
354. Homer, *Iliad* 12.371, 15.439.
355. Homer, *Hymn* 9.4.
356. Horace, *Odes* 1.7, 21–32.

APPENDIX

357. I have brought neither Pylos nor Cyprus into my picture so as not to complicate it unduly by details that had, after all, no decisive influence on the picture described.

Index

I should like, in finishing this manuscript, to thank my son Alexander for all the help he has given me.